Making Room for Students

Sharing Teacher Authority in Room 104

Making Room for Students

Sharing Teacher Authority in Room 104

Celia Oyler

FOREWORD BY D. JEAN CLANDININ

Teachers College, Columbia University
New York and London

Published by Teachers College Press, 1234 Amsterdam Avenue, New York, NY 10027

Library of Congress Cataloging-in-Publication Data

Oyler, Celia.
    Making room for students : sharing teacher authority in Room 104 /
  Celia Oyler ; foreword by D. Jean Clandinin.
      p.   cm.
    Includes bibliographical references (p.   ) and index.
    ISBN 0-8077-3546-9 (cloth : alk. paper). — ISBN 0-8077-3545-0
  (pbk. : alk. paper)
    1. Teacher-student relationships—United States—Case studies.
  2. Interaction analysis in education—United States—Case studies.
  I. Title.
  LB1033.095   1996
  371.1'023—dc20   96-22731
                                             CIP

ISBN 0-8077-3545-0 (paper)
ISBN 0-8077-3546-9 (cloth)

Contents

Foreword by D. Jean Clandinin   vii

Acknowledgments   xi

Introduction   1

1. Entering Room 104   9

   The Context   *9*
   The Development of the Study   *12*
   Dialogic Data Analysis   *15*
   Researcher Positionings and Assumptions   *16*

2. Power, Knowledge, and Shared Authority   19

   Two Dimensions of Teacher Authority   *20*
   Power and Authority   *22*
   Obvious Problematics   *27*

3. "How Come We Haven't Done Any Work Today?":
   Sharing Authority and Classroom Process   31

   Beginning the Day   *32*
   Early Afternoon   *35*
   The Day's End   *40*
   Sharing Authority for Classroom Process   *40*
   Parents' Reactions   *47*

4. "It Gots An Egg": Children's Initiations During
   Teacher-Led Read-Alouds   50

   Teacher Read-Alouds   *50*
   Student Initiations   *51*
   Balancing Teacher Expertise with Student Initiations   *65*

5. "You Could Come Read with Me": Sharing Authority
   in Student-Led Read-Alouds   72

   Journal Read-Alouds   *72*
   Book Read-Alouds   *75*
   Differential Treatment   *83*
   Children's Leadership   *85*

6. "Me and Marcos Know": Negotiating Knowledge
   and Process in Buddy Reading   87

   Shared and Buddy Reading   *87*
   Peer Interactions in Shared Reading   *90*
   Teacher Negotiation of Peer Interaction   *92*
   Putting Down the Books   *95*

7. "That's Not What I Meant": Authorship and
   Authority in Individual Writing   99

   Teacher Authority and Spelling   *99*
   Author Control   *100*
   Journaling: Changes in Genre   *104*
   Journaling: A Social Process   *112*
   At-Home Journals   *114*
   Editing and Revising   *115*

8. "Some Men Make Dinner": Discourse and
   Authority in Teacher-Led Group Writing   117

   Group-Composed Writing   *117*
   Student-Initiated Discourse Pattern   *118*
   Direct Transmission   *124*
   Cued Elicitation   *127*

9. Sharing Authority in the Classroom   132

   Key Aspects of Sharing Authority   *132*
   Looking Beyond   *135*

Afterword by Anne Barry   139
Appendix A: Notes on Method and Methodology   141
Appendix B: Transcription Format   144
References   145
Children's Literature Cited   153
Index   155
About the Author   161

Foreword

On Authority and Co-Authoring

It was a beautiful fall day on the West Coast when I sat down to read Celia Oyler's book, *Making Room for Students: Sharing Teacher Authority in Room 104.* The title intrigued me, and I was prepared to read for an hour or so before I went out to walk by the sea. However, I found myself reading for hours, spellbound not only by the careful writing but also by the provocative ideas Celia develops. This is a wonderful book, a book that makes the ideas of authoring and authority as they shape lives in classrooms come alive.

One of the things a good book does for me is to help me figure out aspects of my own story. If the stories I read resonate with my stories, I can begin to figure out my own practice. As I read Celia's book, the stories that kept welling up in me seemed, at first, to go in two very different ways, one way to teachers' work with children in classrooms and the other to my work as a university administrator researching collaboratively with school administrators.

At first my mind was filled with images of classrooms, of teachers, of children. I imagined Anne Barry, the teacher who worked with Celia, and the children in Room 104 as they worked together to share their writing. As I read about Anne, the children, and Jungman School, I began to think of Monica Donadt, a primary division teacher. The connections I made were not because the schools and the neighborhoods were at all the same. But their images collided in my mind because what Monica and Anne and the children in the two classrooms are trying to do seem much the same. I began to see that they are all trying to learn to share authority. As I read Celia's account of a journal read-aloud where Melinda, a child, and Anne negotiated space with the other children for Melinda's reading, a story Monica wrote came to mind. Monica is concerned to give children space to live out stories of themselves as artists. She wrote:

> Dean, a kindergarten child, announced, as he climbed up on the piano bench, that he would be playing a song for the class. The song did not have a name he calmly said, but it is about music. This exuberant blond-haired young boy confidently began moving his fingers along the keys and singing at the top of his voice. I watched with in-

trigue as he sang with all his heart. His little fingers flew across the keys up and down the piano. The words to his song were not repetitive or predictable. He sang about loving music, about how music fills the air and his piece went on for some time. The rest of the students in the class were not quite sure how to react . . . a few began to look at each other and quietly smile or giggle. I also noticed that they were watching my own reaction closely. . . . I leaned forward with enthusiasm and smiled. This was really amazing. I made eye contact with a few students signalling that it was important to pay attention and then continued to listen and watch intently.

As Dean finished and turned around with a huge smile on his face, he was greeted with a loud round of applause "which we always give in appreciation of performances in our room." . . . It was now time for questions, the usual procedure after someone has shared. I do not remember the first question one of the children asked, but the second one was "Who taught you how to play that song?" Dean answered, "I just know it," and proceeded to sit down. But Michael, a year one student, persisted, "Yes, but did your Dad teach it to you?" "I just learned it," Dean insisted.

Michael was truly impressed with Dean's song and genuinely wanted to know where Dean had learned it. "Yah, but someone must have taught you how to play it," Michael continued. At this point I decided to enter the conversation, "Dean, did you make up that piece on your own?" I asked enthusiastically. At first, he was unsure of how to answer. There was hesitant nod. What was going through his mind? Had I found him out? "Did you know that you are a composer?" I said excitedly. "Dean made that song up all on his own. He is a composer!" (M. Donadt, "A Narrative Study of Art in Teaching" [Master's Thesis, University of Alberta, 1995])

Among the many stories Monica had shared with me, it was this one I remembered as I read of Anne and Melinda's negotiating space. In response to Anne and Melinda's story, Celia wrote:

> This kind of teacher support for students negotiating with peers is a type of expertise that the teacher must delicately balance; without the adequate skills needed to assert her own authority, a child could be overwhelmed by peer comments if the teacher does not provide back-up. Hence an absence of teacher authority here would be considered as an abandonment. Yet for the teacher to intervene too much might close the door to the student learning to do her own negotiation, and it could also stifle future peer input. Thus a large part of teacher expertise in the collaborative classroom is negotiating peer input.

Celia could well have written this in response to Monica's story. And in Celia's response, I saw that Celia named something important in Monica's story, that is, that Monica was trying to share authority with the children. Monica, at the moment when the children began to smile and whisper, entered what Celia would call the dance, "a negotiated dance, where students sometimes lead and the teacher must learn new steps." For Monica, there was uncertainty. What should she do? Would she claim authority as the teacher or would she enter the dance in a way that supported the child as he claimed his authority as an author, a composer? Monica, as did Anne, realized that what she did at any of these possibility-filled moments would make a great difference to the way authority was negotiated in her classroom. Celia's stories of Anne and the children reminded me of Monica and Dean and of the careful dance steps that teachers must take as they negotiate the sharing of authority not only in writing but in the living of classroom stories.

The metaphor of a dance weaves its way evocatively through Celia's text. Celia names three kinds of discourse: transmission discourse, where the teacher is dance instructor; cued elicitation, where the teacher is paid dance partner; and discourse, where the floor is wide open to student initiations, where the dance is a modern one.

As I read the book, my thoughts went to other places, to other dances in which I have engaged. I began to think of other places where I also try to share authority on a professional knowledge landscape, a landscape more accustomed to meta-phorical dance instructors or paid dance partners than such modern dance. My mind filled with images of an ongoing reflective practice group of 12 Canadian school administrators with whom I have participated over a three-year period. While I named myself as collaborator with them as an administrator from a uni-versity landscape rather than a school landscape, I had struggled with how to live a story in which I could join the dance and share authority. While I had entered the group hoping to be collaborative with them, I knew that I was going against the grain of the usual relationship of a university professor with school person-nel. Usually university professors enter as the ones with the authority, as the dance instructor or the paid dance partner. This is, of course, the part university teachers usually play in the sacred theory-driven practice story.

The part I was supposed to play was defined for me at our first meeting, when one of the participants asked me to define the agenda. After a morning of sharing stories, Fred had asked, "What is the agenda for after lunch?" I realized that he was telling me as clearly as he could that as dance instructor or paid dance part-ner, I had the authority. While I had not named it at that moment, now in my re-telling using Celia's language, I realize that it was then that I began to negotiate how to share authority in the group. It was then that I entered the dance. Like Anne and Monica, I began to negotiate the plot line for my story in relation to the others in the group. What I did at that moment made a difference to what happened next.

I realize that in collaborative work with teachers and principals, I, too, am try-ing to dance that modern dance of shared authority. Our group struggled to even-tually come to a place where we lived and told the story as one of shared author-ity, of shared authoring. Three years after Fred's question, the members of our collaborative group, including me, tell our stories as ones in which we negotiated a shared story. Celia's language helps me name the negotiation more clearly as one of sharing authority. While Celia's book speaks to how authority and authoring are shared in classrooms, her work also speaks to many issues of learning to live collaboratively on our professional knowledge landscapes. How had I moved, as Anne had done, from the only one with authority to being one of the ones with authority? This remarkable book raises many new insights into how we construct authority in the many places where we live. Anne, the children in 104, and Celia help us understand this in a compelling way.

D. Jean Clandinin
University of Alberta

Acknowledgments

This book was made possible by the generosity of Anne Barry and her first-grade class of 1991–92. Although I sometimes thought the children must have forgotten my presence in the class (when they were making silent deals behind the teacher's back fully visible to me), they always kept an eye out for what I might need. They offered me samples of their work to photocopy and frequently insisted on filling me in on details I had missed from their days without me. Thank you for your generosity and enthusiasm; it was never boring to sit and listen to your jokes and excitement for learning new things.

I also want to thank the rest of the Jungman school community: parents were friendly, teachers were encouraging, secretaries were helpful, and Fausto Lopez, as principal, invited university collaborators into the school community.

Of course my largest thank-you is to Anne Barry, who welcomed me into her classroom and into her life. Her support over the years has sustained me. Her thinking has challenged me. And her work as a teacher has taught me. Every university researcher should be so fortunate as to have so persistent and patient a teacher-researcher with whom to collaborate.

I want to acknowledge the financial support I received during data collection from the Center for Research in Urban Education and during initial writing from the University Fellowship Program, both at the University of Illinois at Chicago. I want to thank Michelle Mondo and Connie Rinkevage for their assistance throughout the production of this book.

For important feedback on earlier drafts and for teaching me so much, grateful appreciation to Bill Ayers, Sandra Bartky, Victoria Chou, Susan Edgerton, and Bill Schubert.

Mary Manke at National–Louis University paved the way for my work on authority and has generously offered wonderful ideas, an ever-listening ear, and consistent challenge and support.

Joe Becker and Donald Blumenfeld-Jones: thank you.

This work has been sustained and provoked in conversation and friendship with Eileen Ball, Brett Blake, Beth Dohrn, Bill Lamb, Leah Mayers, Margie Mulhern, Mara Sapon-Shevin, and Robin Semer.

Many hearty thanks to Sari Biklen, Kathy Hinchman, and Susan Hynds, colleagues at Syracuse University who have listened to every dilemma and generously offered feedback about this manuscript.

Susan Liddicoat has proved to be a gentle and encouraging editor, with a terrific eye for details and much patience.

This entire project was substantially shaped, guided, and made possible with the careful mentoring and constant friendship of Christine Pappas.

To Jani—who was there through the years of writing and revising—your unwavering support has helped me learn and grow.

Introduction

Marcos,[1] a Mexican American 6-year-old, is sitting on a brown swivel office chair in the front of his urban first-grade classroom reading *Hop on Pop* (Seuss, 1963) out loud to the 23 students in Room 104. The children are quiet and listening, leaning forward to see the pictures that Marcos shows before he turns each page; he makes sure his audience gets to see each picture, moving the book around in a seemingly practiced manner. By the middle of the book, Marcos appears relaxed and confident: He's smiling and making eye contact with his audience as he fluently reads the words on the pages. Marcos certainly has his audience engaged: even Ricky—who rarely attends to large-group activities—is watching and mouthing along with the words.

Near the end of the book, Marcos interrupts his read-aloud and looks directly at Ricky, saying, "Ricky, you could come over here and read with me." Marcos scoots over in the special chair to make room for Ricky, who is up front in a flash. The two readers get to the next page, and now Marcos is watching Ricky intently. Ricky takes the lead and Marcos follows, reading: "My father can read big words, too. Like Constantinople and Timbuktu." They finish *Hop on Pop* and climb down off the chair as the rest of the first graders clap appreciatively. (2/27/92)

I watched this read-aloud from the back of the room in amazement. These 6- and 7-year-olds were not only enjoying reading (both as readers and listeners), but they were *in charge* of the process: Marcos controlling his read-aloud by calling on Ricky to help him; Ricky quickly shifting roles from listener to reader; both of them negotiating the sharing of the special chair, holding the book, and oral reading of the text; and then the audience participating by giving their unprompted rousing round of applause.

Clearly, this is not the typical version of what happens in many first-grade classrooms when children are asked to read out loud. In fact, if I had walked into Anne Barry's classroom a year before, I would have seen the more common routine of

---

1. All children's names are pseudonyms, although the names of the teachers, principal, and school are real.

1

children gathered in a small cluster at the back of the room reading one at a time from their matched set of basal readers, while the rest of the class completed worksheets at their desks. But this year (school year 1991–92), Anne had embarked on a grand experiment she called "holistic" and had radically changed her teaching practice and theories. Influenced by the possibilities afforded by the Chicago School Reform Act of 1988, a master's program, a teacher–university collaborative integrated language arts group, and various readings on emergent literacy, Anne had placed her basals on the shelf. She began to use her extensive collection of previously underutilized children's literature and abandoned many of her traditional teaching routines from the previous 20 years.

The theories Anne Barry has embraced, known as the New Literacy[2] (Willinsky, 1990), and that she calls "whole language," eschew an isolated skills approach and advocate instead that reading and writing are most effectively taught *within* the contexts in which they are naturally used. In this way, Anne set out to create a classroom in which children had real reasons to read and write. To have a real reason to read or write means that the control of the task is turned over in some important ways to the learner. As Willinsky has noted:

> New Literacy programs are intent on altering the meaning of . . . classroom work. . . .
> The shift involves increasing the students' control over the text and its meaning. But to
> shift this meaning of literacy also necessarily alters the relationship between teacher and
> student. The teacher, as an authority on what needs to be known and done, begins to turn
> over more of this responsibility to the student and to the meaning that comes from some-
> where within the student's work with literacy. In these terms, then, the New Literacy's
> proposal is to reshape the *work* of the classroom around a different form of reading and
> writing. The moral, psychological, and social worth of this literacy begins with the stu-
> dents as sources of experience and meaning. To alter the form of literacy in this fashion
> clearly entails redefining the role and relationship of teacher and student. (p. 7)

This idea that teachers can and should turn over some of the responsibility for meaning-making to their students entails utilizing students' experiences and understandings. This is not a common concept, although it is not a new one, either. Almost a century ago, John Dewey called for classrooms in which learning proceeded directly from students' lives. Dewey (1938) called for a "newer school of education" in which "the beginning of instruction shall be made with the experience learners already have" (p. 74).

So, too, has the Brazilian educator, Paulo Freire, made such student-centered inquiry the centerpiece of his education for liberation. He critiques the common

---

2. Willinsky (1990) includes under the umbrella term *the New Literacy* such movements as Whole Language, the Growth Model, Language for Learning, Writing Across the Curriculum, Schema Theory, Reader-Response Theory, Transformational Reading, and the Writing Process Movement.

"banking" model of education in which the teacher is the expert who makes "deposits" of information into the heads of the students. Freire (1970) describes "banking" education this way:

> a) the teacher teaches and the students are taught; b) the teacher knows everything and the students know nothing; c) the teacher thinks and the students are thought about; d) the teacher talks and the students listen—meekly; e) the teacher disciplines and the students are disciplined; f) the teacher chooses and enforces his [sic] choice, and the students comply; g) the teacher acts and the students have the illusion of acting through the action of the teacher; h) the teacher chooses the content and the students, who were not consulted, adapt to it. (p. 59)

Both Freire's and Dewey's critiques of traditional modes of teaching are motivated by the potential for a different kind of education. Rather than seeing students as passive receptacles for teacher knowledge deposits, they propose that education can be a critical underpinning for democracy, empowerment, and liberation. After all, a thriving democracy requires an active citizenry who are producers, not just consumers, of knowledge (Hunter, 1980). Banking modes of education set up students to be consumers of predigested knowledge. In contrast, the New Literacy approaches expect that teachers will start with the assumption that knowledge is not neatly transmittable from individual to individual, but rather is socially constructed. Specifically, the New Literacy or integrated language arts theories assume that (1) learners actively construct their own knowledge; (2) people use language for different purposes in various social contexts, and therefore varying language patterns are realized accordingly; and (3) all learning is social—that is, it is in relation to others and their understandings (Pappas, Kiefer, & Levstik, 1995).

When teachers shape their classrooms around these beliefs, there can be significant consequences for relationships of power and authority between students and teacher. Such an approach, which values learning as a socially constructed process, is facilitated by students assuming a great deal of ownership of classroom work. This, then, requires that teachers renegotiate some of their control over classroom procedures and content. In the words of one teacher, "It takes a great deal of thought, planning and flexibility for a teacher to let students lead and for the teacher to become a demonstrator" (Klein, 1989, p. 191). Some teachers view the issue of control and power-sharing as one of the most difficult aspects of using a collaborative, dialogic (as opposed to didactic, transmission) approach. Regie Routman (1990) addresses this issue from her own experience in the classroom:

> Giving up some control has been my most difficult transition. . . . To gradually move from directing a classroom, where no one speaks without a raised hand and being called upon, to being a colearner in a cooperative environment where students freely express

their opinions was unsettling at first. To slowly change from an environment where all comments are directed to the teacher to a more flexible setting where *students have some choices and respond to one another, as well as to the teacher*, has not happened easily. (p. 24; emphasis added)

The opportunity for students to have choices and respond directly to one another is a part of what I am calling "shared authority" (Oyler, 1996; Oyler & Barry, 1992). Adopting such a teaching stance is fraught with moment-to-moment decisions for teachers regarding when to step *in* and when to step *back*, when to speak as an expert and when to listen to students as they construct their own expertise, and when to direct and when to take up the suggestions of students.

In this book I report on a year-long study in one Chicago first-grade classroom during a year when the teacher was actively reconstructing her pedagogy. As Anne Barry's changes began in the areas of literacy instruction, I examine shared authority in the context of reading and writing, although the underlying issues of knowledge and power can be seen in any curriculum area. It is extremely important, though, to point to the complexities of classroom relationships of authority with teachers who are attempting some of the pedagogies of the New Literacy, such as response-based use of literature and writing-process approaches.

Unfortunately, accounts of these classrooms sometimes skip, or minimize, what Anne refers to as "the bumps" (e.g., Atwell, 1987; Calkins, 1986; Goodman, K., 1986; Graves, 1983; Newman, 1985). Instead what has been presented leaves relationships of authority fairly unproblematized (Lensmire, 1994; Sudol & Sudol, 1991; Willinsky, 1990), and readers build the illusion that their classrooms can be converted into busy hives of productivity and creation if only children are turned free to pursue meaningful tasks. Such portraits, although helpful in terms of theories and practices to support students' literacy acquisition, do not shed light on how shifting the nature of the teacher's role often affects issues of power and authority.

Therefore the notion of sharing authority is developed throughout this book with the desire to offer a tentative framework for thinking about and analyzing relationships of power and authority in classrooms where teachers are attempting progressive pedagogies. By documenting and studying the changes of one teacher with one class of first graders over the course of a school year, I offer an analysis of shared authority between teacher and students. Specifically, I examine the ways in which power has been negotiated for both meaning-making and classroom process. What openings does the teacher provide for students to initiate? What are the questions and dilemmas of the teacher as she negotiates authority? How do students utilize, contest, or reject such a sharing of authority?

As a classroom teacher myself for 15 years, I grappled with ways to create and sustain a community of inquirers and make teaching and learning expansive and emancipatory, rather than oppressive and dominating. Yet within this potentially noble ambition lurks the thorny reality of institutionally maintained forms of teacher power and authority. I propose—and I am certainly not the first educationist to do so—that not only is power not relinquishable, but that it is not always even oppressive. In my study of this one classroom, I argue for a more problematized understanding of classroom power relations than historically has been acknowledged by many progressive pedagogies.

A major premise of this study is that classroom discourse can be analyzed to show how authority is being established, maintained, or negotiated. Numerous studies have shown how teachers traditionally dominate classroom talk and how this domination of the talk also serves to limit and control the flow of knowledge (Cazden, 1988; Edwards, A. D., 1980; Edwards, D., & Mercer, 1987; Forman & Cazden, 1985; Hunter, 1980; Mehan, 1979). Yet we have few in-depth studies of how teachers go about creating classrooms in which they utilize a more collaborative style of teaching. Although exhortations for teachers to create such collaborative classrooms abound in the professional literature, few writers have addressed the shift in power relations that this entails.

Anne's classroom is also important to study because it is an urban one. Because of the deep social/economic inequities in our nation, urban schools are left with few resources, usually large class sizes, frequently hungry and/or malnourished students, low graduation rates, and sometimes low school attendance rates (Kozol, 1991). Additionally, it has been customary in this country to save pedagogies of choice, student-direction, and autonomy for the children of the higher classes (Anyon, 1980; Kohl, 1976; Kozol, 1991) and employ more drill-and-skill (or as some call them: drill-and-kill) and rote learning of basic skills with the children of the urban poor. However, there are classrooms across the United States (and indeed throughout the world) where teachers actively contest such pedagogical constructions for poor children and insist instead on adventurous forms of learning. In these classrooms, children are not seen as "at risk" because their parents are poor or not white. Teachers in such classrooms don't refer to children who have not often traveled out of their own neighborhoods as "experientially deprived." Instead, in classrooms such as Anne Barry's and countless others, teachers actively view children as "at promise" (Swadener & Lubeck, 1995) and willfully construct their classrooms to allow the students' rich "funds of knowledge" (Moll, 1992) into the classroom discourse.

In the process of examining shared authority in this classroom, the skills and expertise of these particular poor, nonmainstream students are made visible. This is not a purely congratulatory account, but one that examines the particular difficulties Anne had as an urban teacher as she attempted to negotiate teaching and learning throughout the year. The research project with Anne and her students turned out to be a joyous one: filled with moments of humor, connection, excitement, and pleasure. Both the teacher and students received me warmly, generously sharing their energy, enthusiasm, and time. They often showed me where to look, calling my attention to things I had missed by being in the classroom only one day a week. They questioned and requestioned my goals and aims: What did I hope to find? What did I think so far? They shared with me their hopes, doubts, fears, triumphs, and personal sorrows. In short, they welcomed me not only into their classroom, but also into their lives.

OVERVIEW OF THE BOOK

Chapter 1 serves as an introduction to this study of shared authority and offers a narrative account of my research. The classroom, school, and neighborhood are described, as well as the various routes that brought Anne Barry and me together for what was in some ways a joint inquiry endeavor. I also explain in some detail the method and methodology of the study, describing ways that Anne and I did and did not share authority for this project.

In Chapter 2 I place shared authority within a theory of power, authority, and knowledge. Although teaching is often used by social science theorists as a classic example of the exercise of power relations (Arendt, 1968; Wartenberg, 1990), few classroom studies have taken on power as a topic of extended study (for exceptions to this, see Gore, 1994, 1995). Certainly some critical theorists have included a microanalysis of power in their theoretical writings (e.g., Bernstein, 1990; Bourdieu & Passeron, 1977), but there is an obvious lack of empirical analyses of classroom power in particular settings. In this chapter I also question the often romanticized versions of some progressive pedagogies that were interpreted by teachers as requiring them to "give up power" and "empower" their students in the classroom. I discuss the nature of teacher authority within the context of progressive pedagogies and speculate (along with Foucault, 1980; Gore, 1993; and Walkerdine, 1990) about the workings of classrooms in moderating well-behaved, self-regulated citizens.

Chapter 3 provides an overview of a typical day in Room 104, taking the reader through the five main literacy routines that are explored in greater detail in each of the following five chapters. Weaving throughout all the chapters—and beginning in Chapter 3—is an exploration of some of the dilemmas and questions Anne grappled with as she began to share authority with her students. A key aspect of this study of shared authority involves examining authority along two dimensions: process and content. When I speak of process, I mean that the teacher is *in* authority for classroom procedures: who gets to do what, where, when, and how. In contrast, the content dimension of authority pertains to the teacher as *an* authority on classroom knowledge: what counts as knowledge and who is validated as a knower. I discuss how these two dimensions are interrelated and negotiated in many educational exchanges in Room 104.

In Chapter 4, I explore student initiations in the context of teacher-led read-alouds. These read-alouds were the centerpiece of Anne's curriculum and in many ways provided the springboard for her next steps in using a literature and process approach to reading and writing. I cover in detail the kinds of initiations the students made, how these changed over the course of the year, how Anne used initiations for assessment and planning, and also the problems inherent in opening the floor to student initiations. In an important way, it was the read-alouds that encouraged Anne to extend her view of shared authority to also include the knowledge, or content, dimension. Frankly, she was stunned by the astuteness, sophistication, and wisdom of the comments children began to make about books and thus connections to the world. This is significant for some urban educators who, too frequently, due to class, race, and cultural differences and prejudices, view urban children as "underprivileged" and "experientially deprived."

In Chapter 5, I turn to a portrayal of shared authority as evidenced in child-led read-alouds—a routine that became more and more frequent as the year progressed. As seen from the introductory excerpt in which Marcos was reading *Hop on Pop* (Seuss, 1963) aloud to the class, students were in control during much of the read-aloud process. The teacher was not a mere audience member. In fact, she played a significant role in the shaping of events, even during a process that appeared at first glance to be mostly in control of the students.

Chapter 6 investigates relationships of authority in another frequent routine in Anne's classroom that she called "buddy reading" or "shared reading." Students chose texts, partners, and locations, often vying for choice seats, preferred peers, or favorite books. Many times they helped each other find a book on a pertinent topic or spent extended periods of time helping each other decode the book. This chapter explores some of the ways students interacted with each other, used each other as resources, and shared authority with the teacher in this classroom routine. Also discussed are some of the struggles Anne encountered regarding monitoring and assessment within a primarily student-to-student routine.

Chapter 7 focuses closely on Anne's dilemmas regarding authority in the area of students' individual writing. In many ways Anne initiated her classroom changes with more advanced plans and confidence in the area of reading than of writing. So in this chapter, Anne has relatively more questions and concerns about her role as teacher and her decisions about sharing authority. A key component in the writing program in Room 104 was the use of children's personal journals. This chapter deals with Anne's ongoing questions about how journals could be most effectively used, particularly regarding when, how, and how frequently she should interact with her students as writers. The process of journal writing changed in some important ways throughout the course of the year, as Anne began to view writing as a social process. By the end of the year, many students talked to one another throughout the journal-writing time. This use of peer collaboration is, again, not commonly seen in many urban classrooms, where some teachers strive for silence and control. (For rich descriptions of urban classrooms utilizing peer collaboration in writing, see Dyson, 1989, 1993.) Thus, by keeping journals and engaging in collaborative, exploratory talk (Barnes, 1990) with peers, students were encouraged to draw upon their personal experiences as a rich source for daily writing.

In addition to new ways of using writing as an individual social process, Anne also used a collaborative style of whole-group writing. Chapter 8, focusing on teacher-led, group-composed writing, offers a chance to examine the co-construction of meaning (Wells & Chang-Wells, 1992) so important in building common understandings over the course of a school year. I propose that it is in the joint construction of knowledge and the shared goal of becoming literate that a sharing of authority even exists. Issues of teacher control are discussed, particularly as related to how the conversational floor was and was not open to student initiations.

However difficult it is to share power and authority in relationships with people as we seek to make sense of the world of education, literacy, and learning, many of us are voyaging into this uncharted water. Chapter 9 concludes with implications and speculations about sharing authority in classrooms and in classroom research. Of particular concern is to explore the colonizing tendencies of teacher authority, particularly when the teacher has emancipatory aims.

In an Afterword, Anne Barry reacts to my account of the study, discusses her latest inquiries and concerns, and shares the particular problems and possibilities of an experienced urban educator. Anne's willingness to look with me at issues of teacher and student authority in pedagogy was a generous and—I would like to propose—bold act. It is not an easy project to interrogate the dominant and dominating forms that limit our own understandings and constrain our knowledge of ourselves and one another. Just as classrooms can be sites of opportunities for student initiations, classroom research can also seek to honor the struggles and stories of teachers determined to carefully investigate their own pedagogy. It is only fitting that this book investigating problems and possibilities of shared authority should conclude with the words of the teacher from Room 104. Throughout the first two years of our work together, Anne referred to teachers as the "not-so-smarts" as compared to university teacher–educators/researchers who were officially recognized as the real authorities. The work of Anne Barry—as shown not only in the Afterword, but throughout this book—actively challenges such deficit constructions of classroom teachers.

1

Entering Room 104

Anne Barry teaches in a Chicago public school classroom where the paint is falling off the walls. Halfway down the block from the old rectangular brick school, over by the elevated railroad tracks, piles of discarded vegetables from the nearby wholesale warehouses rot underneath the bilingual signs: "No tirar basura—No dumping." On my car trips between the nearby university and the school, I often see older people searching through the piles of refuse looking for salvageable food.

THE CONTEXT

At 2:30, when the final bell rings for the day, the doors are flung open, and the mostly dark-haired children in gray uniforms stream out the front door and greet their mothers, grandmothers, sisters, brothers, aunts, and fathers who have gathered there to walk them home. Most of the children and families are speaking Spanish; in fact, 75% of classrooms in this school are called bilingual and use Spanish as the language of instruction, with an increasing amount of English as the students progress through the grades. Most of Anne's Mexican American students are bilingual—two actually speak more Spanish than English—but their parents want them to be in an English-only classroom. Anne's class is the only first-grade monolingual (English) class and has all the students in that grade level whose home language is English.

It's not really only English spoken in class of course. For example, one day I listened as Henry and Felipe sat hunched over a book about Arctic and Antarctic animals discussing penguin behaviors and characteristics in Spanish, although the book was written in English. Felipe received pull-out English as a Second Language instruction, as did Catherine, three times a week; the other students' English proficiency was judged to be sufficient for a monolingual English placement.

The Neighborhood

The neighborhood—called Pilsen—is clearly one where Spanish is the dominant language. When Jungman (pronounced *Young-man*) Elementary was built, Pilsen was a Polish and Lithuanian neighborhood; now it is predominantly Mexican.

9

Chicago has consistently been rated the most segregated city in the United States, and its ethnically and racially marked neighborhoods bear witness to this fact. Walking down the streets of Pilsen can almost feel like Mexico according to one of my homesick Mexican friends who came from Vermont to visit me in Chicago; Mauricio was able to get warm corn tortillas filled with grilled meat from a rotating spit ("tacos al pasteur"), read books in Spanish at Rudy Lozano Library, and wander the streets admiring numbers of vibrant street murals depicting political and cultural themes.

Pilsen is only one of Chicago's neighborhoods where Spanish is a language of commerce, home, and school. In the 1991–92 school year, there were more than 40,000 Spanish-speaking children participating in bilingual programs in the Chicago public schools (Chicago Public Schools, 1992–93). Although store signs and graffiti are often written in Spanish, Pilsen is also home to many young gringo artists in search of inexpensive housing in a neighborhood untouched by gentrification. These small, often badly maintained, apartments also provide affordable rents to large extended families of recent rural Mexican immigrants, particularly from the state of Michoacán. Residents' ties to Mexico are strong; in the nine months I spent in Anne's class, at least two children visited relatives in Mexico. Yet there are also Mexican American families who have lived in the neighborhood for generations; when I interviewed parents, three of them told me they had attended Jungman School themselves.

Pilsen is one of many Chicago neighborhoods plagued by gang violence, school overcrowding, and grinding poverty. Potholes and rubble often fill the streets, and there is little green to alleviate the endless expanse of brick, concrete, and asphalt. Surrounded on two sides by highways, and on a third by a series of warehouses, the neighborhood does not even seem to shelter many squirrels or birds; on a trip to the zoo in the spring, the first graders in Anne Barry's class were as excited by the wild robins as by the animals in cages.

The School and Chicago School Reform

Children at Jungman, though, are not all Mexican or Mexican American. In Anne Barry's class, for example, Celina is Puerto Rican, Montrel and LaToya are African American, Lola is European American, and Maya and Camila have one Latina parent and one Anglo parent. Although their ethnic backgrounds differ, the children at Jungman school all come from low-income families. In fact, in the 1991–92 school year, 100% of the students in the school lived in families with incomes below federally determined poverty levels (Jungman School Team, 1992). Schooling and socioeconomic status are correlated in the United States, but even so, nearly 70% of neighborhood students never graduate from high school (Jungman School Team, 1992).

Jungman is a neighborhood school and often loses children who are able to gain admittance to the magnet schools scattered throughout the city. In fact, it is in part because of the magnet schools that Jungman's school population does not include the children of more financially stable families who live in Pilsen. Parents with knowledge and/or connections work to enroll their children in magnet schools, either by test or by lottery. In either case, it is typically the more privileged parents who manage to get their children into these special schools.

Chicago magnet schools were created in large part to stem the "white flight" of the 1960s, when large numbers of middle-class families moved to the suburbs. Although certainly a benefit to many children, the magnet schools have the side effect of draining the neighborhood schools of many of their most vocal, active, schooled, and connected parents. Thus the resources these families typically give to their children's schools are not available for neighborhood schools such as Jungman. This is not to imply that Jungman parents are not involved in their children's school, because there is much evidence of parental activity around the school. In large part because of parental control of the Local School Council (LSC) and a thriving Parents' Center with a full-time coordinator, parents are always in the building, often in classrooms, and involved in general school affairs. On many of the days I spent in Anne's class, mothers stopped by to help out in the class or just to browse around the room and watch what their children were doing.

The year 1991 was also the beginning of the third year of Chicago school reform, a process that fostered some structural and curricular changes at Jungman. Since the Chicago School Reform Act of 1988 (P.A. 85-1418), all schools in Chicago were required to have a Local School Council with parents, teachers, and community members making a long-range plan for the school and appointing the school principal. Jungman's LSC was quite active and often sponsored assemblies and community meetings; they were vigorous in setting school policies, voting, for example, to require the gray school uniforms: skirts for girls and pants for boys.

Fausto Lopez, Jungman's principal, was also active in making connections to school reform projects. His school was chosen to participate in the federally funded five-year Project CANAL (Creating A New Approach to Learning), focused on site-based planning. Mr. Lopez acted as an instructional leader by, among other things, bringing in consultants on new approaches to literacy and instituting schoolwide procedures to prepare for standardized achievement tests. A native of Ecuador fluent in both Spanish and English, Mr. Lopez had the support of local parents on the LSC. He also was successful in negotiating with the central office bureaucrats, which enabled Jungman to be the recipient of numerous reform-oriented programs. If the opportunity existed for money and resources, Fausto Lopez knew how to get it.

Meeting the Teacher

One reform project Jungman School was hooked into—"The Network"—involved the University of Illinois at Chicago; funded by the Center for Research in Urban Education, university education professors provided Network schools a range of services as requested. A group of Jungman teachers, intrigued by a presentation on "whole language," used Network connections to invite Christine Pappas, a university teacher educator, to talk to them about using an "integrated language approach" (Pappas et al., 1995). As a doctoral research assistant in what became a long-term collaboration, I went along with Chris as she met with a group of about 10 women teachers (including Mexican Americans, a Cuban American, an African American, and European Americans) once a week during the spring semester of 1991.

Chris negotiated with the teachers to engage in collaborative research with teachers making instructional changes in urban schools. In this context I conducted audiotaped interviews with the participating teachers and had the first of many extended conversations with Anne Barry, a member of the teachers' group.

Anne grew up in a white, working-class neighborhood on the southwest side of Chicago. Her mother was widowed when Anne was 2 years old and was a city school teacher all her life. Anne also has been an urban teacher for her entire career; in 1991, she was in her twentieth year of teaching in Chicago public schools. Anne had taken a few years off while her four children were young, but quickly returned to the classroom. Anne now lives in a western suburb but is fiercely committed not only to urban education in general but to neighborhood schools in particular. She won't even consider applying for a job at a magnet school, where conditions are usually much better for both teachers and students. Anne was deeply involved in the business of classroom change and school reform: She had been elected chair of Jungman's Project CANAL core planning team and in 1991 enrolled in an intensive M.Ed. program at National–Louis University.

THE DEVELOPMENT OF THE STUDY

In the university–school collaborative teachers' group one afternoon, a teacher posed a question that began to express for me the specific issue of shared authority. A fifth-grade teacher related a dilemma of one Monday morning. José walked into class with a burning question on his mind: "Teacher," he asked her, "Why the rainbow 'round the moon?" Not knowing a quick answer to why when we look at the moon sometimes there appear to be rings of color around it, Ms. Freidman debated whether to encourage José to go and research the question immediately or to put the topic on hold and direct him to finish the play script his group was writing. In her old style of a more rigidly controlled curriculum, she probably would not have felt José's question as a dilemma, as student initiations did not play a main role in curriculum development. Now, though, somewhat persuaded that learners' questions, interests, and initiations can be a foundation of classroom instruction, Ms. Freidman puzzled over how to use her authority as teacher.

I had already encountered the phrase "sharing of authority" (Tierney & Rogers, 1989, p. 255) to describe classroom occasions when students were permitted to take a more authoritative role. In fact, I was still teaching part time that semester (while also a full-time doctoral student and a part-time graduate assistant) and had designed a small study of the talk in my own classroom during activities designed to promote student-to-student talk—what Jay Lemke (1990) has termed "cross-discussion." In this study, I analyzed whether the typical IRE pattern had been replaced and, if so, what had taken its place. In this commonly recognized form of classroom discourse, IRE, the teacher Initiates by asking a question, the student Responds, and then the teacher Evaluates the student's answer or comment (Cazden, 1988; Mehan, 1979). The net effect of such a pattern is that teacher talk dominates most classrooms by a two-thirds margin (Edwards, D., & Mercer, 1987).

In my own classroom research, I had documented the ways that my high school students initiated talk during instructional events. In examining the types of initiations they made, I realized that many initiations could be characterized as process-type comments or questions. That is, students either gave directions or asked questions about what to do next or how to do it. The other broad category I noticed was what I called "content initiations." These two types of initiations are what I began to see as two distinct but intertwined dimensions of authority. Of course, this is not news. In 1966, Peters wrote about teachers being *in* authority to accomplish the task of teaching and *an* authority regarding some aspect of our culture. If teacher authority can have a process and a content dimension, then, of course, these authorities can be shared with students.

I brought this agenda of mine that I was now calling "shared authority" to the meetings of the teachers' group when they resumed in September 1991. At the end of the first semester (May 1991), some of the teachers and both university researchers had decided to continue working together for the next school year. As part of the negotiation, teachers agreed to consider having one or both of the university researchers in their classrooms to research their instructional changes. I approached Anne Barry and also a third-grade teacher and asked if they would be interested in investigating the issue of shared authority in depth; I chose these two because the other teachers used Spanish almost all day and I do not speak much Spanish. They both agreed, and I began visiting the classrooms in October, spending one full day a week in each room. I acted as a participant–observer, sometimes joining classroom activities but most commonly sitting at the back of the room taking field notes. From the very beginning I brought my tape recorder and an external microphone and recorded classroom talk.

In all classroom research projects there are numerous decisions to be made regarding where to focus, how to look and listen, and what to leave out. There is so much to notice in all classrooms, but this is exacerbated in classrooms where teachers strive for more collaborative relations; more often than not, many people are talking at once and students are frequently pursuing different tasks. So it must be understood that I had decided in advance of entering the classrooms that I was interested in examining relationships of authority as realized in the classroom discourse. Therefore this work is not an ethnographic account of life in one classroom, nor a phenomenological study of the participants' perspectives. I also did not set out to paint a portrait of exemplary teaching or create a model that could be replicated by other teachers. Rather, I have used classroom discourse analysis and ethnographic techniques to analyze and theorize about a particular topic: shared authority. In this way, then, this project could be termed a topic-oriented ethnographic study (Hymes, 1982) using classroom discourse.

During the months of October, November, and December, I cast a rather large net and tape-recorded a variety of instructional events, particularly focusing on teacher-led activities. These large-group activities provided opportunities for me to hear the negotiations between students and teachers that I was interested in analyzing for underlying relationships of power and authority. In January the third-grade teacher was "reassigned" to a position as a floating ESL teacher, and she decided not to have me observe her.

By January, after documenting and observing the various routine activities in Anne's classroom, I decided to focus on the specific routines covered in this book: teacher-led read-alouds; student-led read-alouds; shared reading; journal writing; and teacher-led group writing. Although issues of shared authority could certainly be explored in any instructional event, these five were not only regular routines but were also areas about which Anne was most eager to explore the topic of authority. As her comments and questions most frequently revolved around the areas of literacy, I decided to focus on the specific components of her literacy program. Shared reading was the only activity in which I was more often a participant than an observer. This is because students deluged me with requests to read with them, and on many occasions their sheer enthusiasm persuaded me to put down my pen and do so. (Most often what they meant by "read with" was to listen and help with words they wanted to know.)

From the very beginning, I had no trouble finding instances of student initiations; these became topics of discussion between Anne and me during her 20-minute lunch break or after school. These conversations were also recorded, as were informal conversations we had before and after the weekly teachers' meeting. Additionally, we often spoke on the telephone while I took notes of these conversations. Other sources of data from classroom visits include the following: photographs of written material posted on the chalkboard and around the room; collections of student writing that they volunteered to let me photocopy; and letters and notes students sent to me. (See Appendix A for further details on methodology.)

DIALOGIC DATA ANALYSIS

Many of the traditional boundaries between researcher and researched were blurred as Anne and I puzzled together over the shifting patterns of control, both for classroom process as well as the construction of knowledge in her class. Rather than distance and objectivity as a researcher, I aimed for closeness and disclosure. I did not try to keep my perceptions private; instead I viewed this study as a collaborative one in which we attempted to make meaning and sense together. John Heron (1981) states the importance of this position clearly:

> Persons, as autonomous beings, have a moral right to participate in decisions that claim to generate knowledge about them. . . . Knowledge fuels power: it increases the efficacy of decision-making. Knowledge about persons can fuel power *over* persons or fuel power *shared with* persons. And the moral principle of respect for all persons is most fully honored when power is shared not only in the application of knowledge about persons, but also in the generation of such knowledge. (pp. 34–35)

This study of sharing authority in Anne's classroom is also a study in which I as researcher attempted to share authority with Anne, not viewing her as a bug under a microscope but treating her as a co-investigator in the project. Of course, there are inherent tensions and dilemmas in such an approach, not unlike the ones teachers face as they attempt such a sharing of authority with their students (Oyler & Pappas, 1992).

This dialogic process between Anne as teacher and me as researcher represents a fundamental shift in educational research, which has been dominated by notions of control and prediction arising from the positivist paradigm of the natural sciences (Lather, 1991). Some educational researchers are turning away from such approaches, embracing instead methods and methodologies that seek to listen to teachers and students as they make meaning. Such research is not new, however, having roots at least as far back as the laboratory school of Alice Chipman Dewey and her husband John Dewey (Cremin, 1961). The Deweys advocated that schools become scientific laboratories where children and teachers could reflect on their experiences to reach new understandings. Later Lewin (1944), and then Stenhouse (1975), extended this notion of collaborative inquiry, developing methods of action-research which based investigations *within* their social contexts and linked research with social change.

Feminist university-based researchers have in recent accounts been struggling with ways to highlight the voices and perspectives of the teachers with whom they work. These efforts have included using the reflections of teachers as a center-

piece of narrative accounts (Miller, 1990); subjecting reflections and interpretations to a dialogic, interactive process (Johnston, 1990); following teachers' own
agendas and questions in the research question and development (Gitlin, 1990);
and co-authoring with teachers (Clandinin, Davies, Hogan, & Kennard, 1993;
Edelsky, Draper, & Smith, 1983; Hollingsworth & Minarik, 1991). These accounts
of teachers' questions in their own voices help bring an essential and long-missing
perspective to university-based educational research and change.

Collaborative theorizing with teachers shifts the location of knowledge about
teaching and children from outside the school classroom to *inside* the classroom,
in much the same way that the New Literacy (Willinsky, 1990) philosophies
shift knowledge location from outside the child to a process of classroom interaction that values the experiences and understandings of students as they enter
the classroom. In collaborative inquiry, researchers and teachers both contribute
to "hypothesis-making, to formulating the final conclusions, and to what goes on
in between" (Heron, 1981, p. 19). As R. Young (1992) has pointed out, educational research has failed teachers by dismissing their knowledge; teachers should
be involved in research as participants and part of the validation process—not just
as data. Thus this study respects teachers' personal, practical knowledge (Connelly
& Clandinin, 1990) and relies heavily on collaborative theorizing (see Ayers &
Schubert, 1992; Gitlin, 1990; Hollingsworth, Teel, & Minarik, 1992; Johnston,
1990; Miller, 1990).

Even though I have shared every piece of writing with Anne and asked her to
give me feedback, this is still one version of reality: my own. If Anne herself had
written this book, it would be a different one, perhaps focusing on other events or
arriving at different conclusions. Although the question of authority was indeed a
mutual one and our process was open, honest, trusting, and exciting, we have since
acknowledged that we both wanted more opportunities to sift through the data,
speculate, discuss, and make our conclusions together. After the year I spent in
Anne's class, we have written and presented papers together at national conferences (Oyler & Barry, 1992, 1993), and Anne has written an Afterword for this
book; these collaborative writing projects have certainly furthered our discussions
on this and other topics. But I do want to note that it is difficult and worrisome to
share authority in the research process. Certainly the schedules of university researchers and school teachers are not the same, nor are the reward structures for
conducting and writing up such research.

RESEARCHER POSITIONINGS AND ASSUMPTIONS

Each day that I entered Anne's classroom and worked on this research project, I
brought my (sometimes shifting) positionings and assumptions with me. Rather
than pretend that I was "objective"—something I did not want to be—I will out-

line some of the filters through which this study passed. First, I am a teacher and have been one for the last 15 years. If asked before this project, I would have said I knew a fair amount of what was going on in my classroom. So sitting in Anne's class, I was quite surprised by how much was said by students in the course of a school day to which the teacher was never privy. Some of these exchanges have been included in the data. Others presented me with ethical dilemmas regarding how much I should reveal to Anne. I felt strongly that even though my very presence in the room was changing the environment and interactions, thereby changing learning and teaching in the classroom, I did not want to act as a "spy" for the teacher, highlighting student actions she did not see.

Second, my only language is English, and the majority of the students in Anne's class were also fluent in Spanish. Although I have been learning Spanish for many years, there were conversations among students that I did not understand. Furthermore, although I have lived in neighborhoods with low-income people for many years, I am comfortably middle-class. The students at Jungman, however, are all eligible for federal free lunches (Chicago Public Schools, 1992). These social-class differences also can result in different language understandings (Heath, 1983).

Third, my assumption regarding language is that it is social and situational and can therefore not be detached from the context in which it occurs. So obvious limitations are inherent in this study: I was an outsider to the neighborhood as well as absent for the majority of school days throughout the year. Furthermore, I was an observer of events, not a main actor in them.

Fourth, I am a woman. Being a woman situated me closer to Anne in that I gained her confidence on a personal level; I was privy to some of the outside pressures in her life that were part of her own context as a teacher. But because of this closeness, there are things that I will not reveal in a public record.

In many ways, Anne and I work well together because we share the common agenda of shaping schools into sites of possibility rather than passivity. We are also both committed to doing this in poor neighborhoods. As we open up the classroom floor to student initiations, we realize that when students are allowed to initiate in areas of literacy, they will initiate in other areas as well, presenting new problems for teachers as they share their authority. This is particularly important when working with students whose parents are not part of the mainstream culture of power (Delpit, 1988). As Anne stated: "It's the world's perception of minority kids that doesn't really allow for the opening up of the kids' funds of knowledge. I'm driving the curriculum, and I want to give them a fighting chance."

There is an important link, then, between critical literacy and the power to act upon the world. As Giroux (1988) has noted:

> [Literacy is] the precondition for engaging in struggles around both relations of meaning and relations of power. To be literate is *not* to be free, it is to be present and active in the struggle for reclaiming one's voice, history, and future. (p. 65)

This was a classroom where the teacher actively sought to share *some* author-ity *sometimes* with students because of her desire for them to acquire critical lit-eracy skills. Becoming literate and actively initiating in the classroom for both content and process do not mean that students are free. They are not free from the constraints of order inherent in any institution; their teacher is not free to imagine that the students do not live marginalized lives and have unproblematic futures. Yet these constraints need not prevent the students from making their voices heard and their desires known. They only serve to make the work of teachers and stu-dents that more urgent and important.

2

Power, Knowledge, and Shared Authority

> Last year when I started my whole adventure in learning holistic philosophies, when I did [small group projects with the students] that to me was a huge step in my losing—not losing power, but changing of it. . . . It was terrifying. Terrifying is not the right word. I was really scared of it. (Anne Barry, 11/8/91)

Central to the notion of shared authority is the context of pedagogical change. As Anne expressed above, when teachers implement holistic, or progressive, or New Literacy (Willinsky, 1990) approaches, relationships of power and authority are often challenged and altered. This chapter provides a theoretical framework for shared authority by exploring issues of power and knowledge in classroom and pedagogical relations.

Even though Anne had been teaching for 20 years when she embraced "holistic" methods, she was worried about the effects these changes would have on her authority in the classroom. In her years of traditional teaching, Anne's students had used basals and workbooks as the mainstay of their literacy curriculum. Anne's decisions about instruction and planning were determined in large part by publishing companies, as articulated in the teachers' manuals. The underlying belief she was operating from was that classrooms are sites of knowledge transmission; the teacher is the transmitter of this knowledge, and the textbook companies make decisions about sequence and content.

As Anne learned more about the theories of the New Literacy (Willinsky, 1990), she became convinced that students are active constructors of knowledge, based on experience and prior understandings. Thus Anne decided to change the form of her instruction to allow for more dialogic, rather than didactic (Hunter, 1980), pedagogical processes. Educational theorists have labeled this distinction between a transmission and a constructivist approach in a variety of ways, as can be seen in Table 2.1. These categories, grouped as either "progressive" or "traditional," are binary categories and therefore tend to obfuscate the actual continuous range of such orientations. These classifications should be viewed as different ends of a continuum along which real teachers in their actual classroom practice will often

TABLE 2.1. Vocabulary of Binary Distinctions in Teaching

Traditional	Progressive	Author
Banking	Liberatory	Freire (1970)
Didactic	Dialectic	A. D. Edwards (1980)
Didactic	Dialogic	Hunter (1980)
Cold science	Hot science	Delamont (1983)
Teacher as instructor	Teacher as facilitator	Doake (1985)
Transmission	Transaction	Wells (1986)
Transmission	Interpretive	Barnes (1990)
Power over	Power with	Kreisberg (1992)
Method classroom	Discourse classroom	R. Young (1992)

be at different spots, depending on the nature of the activity, the teacher's mood, the children's interactions, the teacher's goals, and so forth. Thus these binary distinctions are not meant to be rigid; rather they are included to sharpen the distinction between transmission versus more collaborative styles of teaching. Additionally, such categories help connect the various terms that have been used to describe a more progressive style of teaching in which power and control are shared in important ways with students.

TWO DIMENSIONS
OF TEACHER AUTHORITY

In traditional modes of teaching, authority is not often a problematic concept. The teacher is expected to maintain it, and students are supposed to respect it. It is only in the move toward more dialogic pedagogies involving negotiations of knowledge and power that sharing authority even arises as a possibility or concern. As teachers make room for student initiations, they invite a different form of classroom interaction. Anne noticed the difference opening the floor to student initiations made when she explained in December 1991: "I've never had kids give me things like this before. I would never know how much they know if I didn't allow this level of interaction. I'm sorry I never did it before."

Anne's comment points to the dual nature of teacher authority; she first references the kinds of knowledge that children are able to express, and then she explains that this knowledge is allowed into the classroom by the level of interaction that she has permitted. This is an excellent illustration of the two sides of teacher authority, as well as the integral connection between them. As Peters (1966) noted: A teacher is *an* authority regarding some aspect of our culture and is *in* authority to accomplish the task of teaching. Essentially, the former side of authority is a content dimension—what counts as knowledge and who is a "knower"; whereas the latter is more of a process dimension—controlling the flow of traffic and of talk in the classroom. Thus teacher authority has both a content dimension (what counts as knowledge) and a process dimension (who gets to do what, where, when, and how). These, of course, are interwoven and interdependent. According to Stubbs (1976), "There is no way in which maintaining social control and transmitting knowledge can be strictly separated. In the classroom, we have a quite specific case where 'knowledge is power'" (p. 95).

One of the principal means for deploying power and circulating knowledge in classrooms is through talk. As Carlsen (1991) notes, "Classroom talk reflects and reinforces differences in social status and authority between teachers and students" (p. 171). This talk, which reflects and structures relationships of authority about classroom process and status, also performs the same sort of structuring and reflecting regarding knowledge construction. In most classrooms around the world, two-thirds of the time is spent talking, and teacher talk dominates by a two-thirds majority (Delamont, 1983; Flanders, 1970). Teachers also dominate classroom talk in other ways as well: They allocate turns and speaking rights, they evaluate the answers to questions they have posed, and they interrupt students freely (Cazden, 1988; Edwards, A. D., & Mercer, 1987; Lemke, 1990; Mehan, 1979). Teachers frequently use *sequences* of questions to maintain tight control of discourse topics (Farrar, 1988). These questions, unlike questions in most conversations outside of classrooms, are pseudo-questions (Barnes, 1990) to which the teacher already knows the answer. Used in this way, teachers' questions represent a tool of evaluation regarding the correctness of the student responses and are therefore not genuine questions, but test questions.

Dillon (1985), in his study of classroom talk in five secondary classrooms, demonstrated how teachers' questions actually limit discussion, whereas noninterrogative comments serve to facilitate lengthier, more syntactically complex responses in students. This conclusion is supported in the work of Wood and Wood (1988), who note that "the more teachers question students, the less initiative they show and the less they say" (p. 294). Alpert (1987) found that the most active student participation took place in classrooms where teachers' questions were more interpretational, rather than factual; teachers did not evaluate responses; and teachers did not allocate speaking turns.

Thus teachers' control of their classes that is designed to maintain order also serves to control the flow of knowledge and limit the participation of students (Edwards, D., 1980; Hunter, 1980). However, in classrooms where teachers share control, different patterns have been noted. There are more student-selected and self-selected speakers—students call on one another more, or nominate themselves (Edwards, 1980). There are more student-initiated questions and evaluations, along with a dominance of substantive talk about texts (Tierney & Rogers, 1989). And finally, when given the opportunity to do so, students take a more significant part in steering the route of discussion (Christie, 1989).

This connection between controlling the classroom and controlling the knowledge flow was noted by Stenhouse (1975) in a project he directed that aimed at changing the stance of teacher from deliverer of curriculum to mediator and questioner. Opening up the curriculum resulted in exacerbating issues of discipline and control for the teachers involved. In the weekly teachers' group, Anne and her colleagues also frequently discussed issues of control that arose for them when they allowed students more freedom to move around the room and interact with their peers. It can be argued, then, that control over knowledge and control over conduct are inextricably linked. Perhaps the role of the teacher illustrates the connection between power and knowledge more vividly than any other institutional position. It is in school that the child is brought from the private realm of the home and family into the social world (Grumet, 1988). It is the teacher's job to use her or his knowledge and power to bring the student into the public sphere of the knowing and acting.

POWER AND AUTHORITY

Researchers investigating issues of power in education have come from a variety of perspectives. Jennifer Gore (1994) has categorized the variety of perspectives educational researchers have used in writing about power. They are as follows:

> (1) Technical—seeking techniques to ensure a "correct" balance between teacher and student power; (2) organisational—seeking to understand the functioning of power at the level of the bureaucratic institution; (3) ideological—seeking to reveal, through ideology critique, the capitalist, patriarchal, racist practices and effects of schooling and to provide visions of alternative pedagogies aimed at transforming classroom and societal power relations; and (4) empowering—seeking to shift the balance of power in educational systems and institutions. (p. 2)

This study and analysis in Anne Barry's class does not fit exactly into any of the above categories, although certainly one of the aims of the project is to portray possible alternative pedagogies in actual practice. However, an examination of how authority is negotiated or shared could be conducted in any classroom—not just in a classroom where the teacher is actively attempting to change her pedagogy. Such an analysis depends on a theory of power as productive and relational (Foucault, 1980; Gore, 1993; Kreisberg, 1992; Walkerdine, 1990; Wartenberg,

1990). That is, rather than attempt to portray power as a possession mainly of teacher, and sometimes of students, an analysis of shared authority depends on a view of power as always realized among participants through the discourses (not only the talk). In this way, power and authority are created and maintained through interactions, not held as possessions. Foucault (1980) explains:

> Power must be analyzed as something which circulates, or rather as something which only functions in the form of a chain. It is never localized here or there, never in anybody's hands, never appropriated as a commodity or piece of wealth. Power is employed and exercised through a net-like organization. And not only do individuals circulate between its threads; they are always in the position of simultaneously undergoing and exercising this power. They are not only its inert or consenting target; they are always also the elements of its articulation. In other words, individuals are the vehicles of power, not its points of application. (p. 98)

This conception of authority means that for a teacher to share authority is not like sharing a cookie, where if half is given away, only half is left. Rather, when a teacher shares authority, power is still being deployed and circulating, but perhaps in different—and potentially more covert—ways.

If individuals are the vehicles of power, how we are driving matters a great deal. Here, Seth Kreisberg's (1992) notion of *power with*, versus *power over*, is helpful. As teachers strive toward positions of *power with* students, they develop relations of "co-agency . . . characterized by people finding ways to satisfy their desires and to fulfill their interests without imposing on one another" (pp. 85–86). If a teacher is planning destinations, selecting routes, determining speed, and discussing pit stops *with* the students, then this is a relationship in which important decisions are not made by the teacher alone. Sharing authority, then, is much more than just offering activity choices; rather, it requires that teacher and students develop and negotiate a common destination or agenda.

Abdicating or Claiming Authority

There are inherent tensions regarding power and knowledge between the traditional role of teacher as authority and the progressive possibility of shared authority and co-construction of meaning (Wells & Chang-Wells, 1992). The first tension involves the process of sharing power with students and can be seen in many radical educators' interpretations of progressive pedagogies. In critiquing and rejecting the position of teacher as authoritarian boss and dominator, some progressive educators shun teacher authority as an evil. In this way of thinking, power is seen as repressive and should always be avoided. This kind of analysis of teacher authority leads to a set of familiar dichotomies: teacher-centered versus student-centered curriculum, structured versus unstructured classrooms, and authoritarian versus laissez-faire approaches to discipline. In an attempt to avoid repressing and subjugating students, teachers attempt to move out of students' way. Thus, in the rejection of the hard place of authoritarianism, teachers move to the other side of the dichotomy: to the soft place of abdicated authority (Oyler & Becker, 1993). For example, Ira Shor recommends: "In a liberatory classroom, the teacher seeks to gradually withdraw as the director of the learning, as the directive force" (Shor & Freire, 1987, p. 90). So in the soft place, directivity, structure, and authority are to be withdrawn. The teacher is urged to (metaphorically) leave the room—turning over control to students.

Abdicated teacher authority has its roots in a belief that since power is repressive, children will best develop personal voice and creativity if freed from teacher restrictions. As Jesse Goodman (1992) has noted in regard to many radical educators:

> Freedom is viewed as the absence of external control over the individual. . . . The emphasis often is on simplistic rejection of that which is "bad," such as formal knowledge, skills, authority, or structure, and praise for that which is "good," such as individual freedom, creativity, or decision making. (p. 27)

The soft place, then, is the romantic garden where children, if left to their own devices, will develop naturally into self-regulated, creative individuals. This is the belief system that underlies many interpretations (or misinterpretations) of whole-language and writing-process approaches (Luke, 1991). Such approaches tend to hide relations of power between teacher and students, as well as among students (Willinsky, 1990). This is, of course, a great danger for those who seek to critique and change the status quo. To be transformative, pedagogies must work to reveal and challenge existing social hierarchies (Edelsky, 1991). This requires active and engaged teachers who not only problematize their positions of authority, but also claim their expertise in collaboration with their students (Oyler & Pappas, 1992). This position of teachers claiming authority is a different place from either the hard place of teacher authoritarianism or the soft place of abdicated authority. It is not a conceptually familiar place. According to Manke (1991), "A radical break with what is ordinarily taken-for-granted," is called for, and the teacher "must place herself on a level with the students as co-investigators of the problems to be posed" (p. 5). Thus the teacher is not absent: She or he is co-investigating with students. But I would add to Manke's assertion that teachers can *pose* as co-investigators with students but are not able to be on the "same level" due to institutional hierarchies and practices that we work within. We must move toward collaborative forms of inquiry, but we will not dissolve the status and privileges that accrue from our positions.

In any case, this "radical break" is no easy disruption. A teacher's job requires that she assume full responsibility for classroom process and students' learning—

she must accept her authority and use it to structure the classroom. As teachers struggle to carefully scaffold (Bruner, 1985; Vygotsky, 1978; Wood, Bruner, & Ross, 1976) their students' learning, the very role of teachers and their authority gets called into question. It is a difficult balance to both assume responsibility for learning and at the same time attempt to scaffold students' abilities as they begin to assume some of their own responsibility to learn.

Claiming authority and expertise should not be conflated with what some critical theorists term "emancipatory authority" (Giroux & McLaren, 1986). This approach insists that teachers "specify the political and moral referents for authority they assume in teaching particular forms of knowledge, in taking stands against forms of oppression, and in treating students as if they ought to be concerned about social justice and political action" (p. 226). Emancipatory pedagogy demands that the teacher knows (or believes he knows) how to empower or liberate the learner. This is captured by Paulo Freire (Shor & Freire, 1987) in his explication of the difference between authority and authoritarianism:

> For me the question is not for the teacher to have less and less authority. The issue is that the democratic teacher never, never transforms authority into authoritarianism. He or she can never stop being an authority or having authority. Without authority it is very difficult for the liberties of the students to be shaped. (p. 91)

Freire, here, does not go to the soft place of abdicated authority. He wants to distinguish between authority and authoritarianism but may be conflicted about how to do this, for at the end, he seems to infer that the liberties of the students need to be shaped by the teacher. Certainly students deserve the teacher to be fully present and available with her expertise. However, it is problematic to assume that the self-critical emancipatory teacher can liberate students in the classroom (Ellsworth, 1989). The teacher who attempts to share authority for classroom process and knowledge cannot ever fully know students' lives, experiences, values, and needs. Therefore, all knowledge of the students must always be partial and tentative, and the teacher's moves toward claiming authority and expertise must be partial also.

Individual or Co-Constructed Meaning

In addition to the tension arising from the move toward the soft place of abdicated authority, there is another significant problem regarding the move toward progressive pedagogies. It arises in large part because of the individualistic nature of much of our theorizing about teaching, learning, child development, and, for that matter, democracy. Much of the critique of transmission teaching has arisen from advocates of discovery learning, or child-centered approaches, such as the British Primary School movement (Plowden, 1967). These learning theories—based originally in large part around the work of Piaget—are developmental and individual, with the teacher retaining control over knowledge (Edwards, D., & Mercer, 1987; Goodman, 1992; Wells & Chang-Wells, 1992). The child is seen as an increasingly independent learner who uses language to express thought. Such theories, although useful for their work in individual cognition, do not place the learner within the *social* and interactional context of the classroom. According to Wells and Chang-Wells (1992), in discovery learning:

> The learner is seen . . . as independent and self-contained, and learning activities as taking place *within* individuals rather than in transactions *between* them. Furthermore, because knowledge—whether learner constructed or teacher-transmitted—is taken in both ideologies to be an individual possession . . . little attention is given to the task-related discourse in which knowledge is collaboratively constructed, validated, and modified in the purposeful activities in which learners engage with others in the cultural communities of home or school. (p. 28)

It is this collaborative construction of knowledge that is highlighted and actively built upon when teachers share authority with students in the classroom. Of course in all classrooms—and indeed outside of classrooms also—people collaboratively construct knowledge, whether or not teachers share authority with students. For instance, among the working-class students in the English secondary school studied by Paul Willis (1977), students constructed identities and meanings for themselves in contrast to the officially sanctioned school knowledge being transmitted. Students who do not go along with the teacher's agenda are sometimes said to be "resisting": either resisting authority or resisting "liberatory" curricula. So, too, could students who declare their intentions not to share authority with a teacher be viewed as resisting the teacher's pedagogy.

Regardless of what students do in response to teachers who actively attempt to share authority for classroom process and knowledge, such pedagogy invites a co-construction of meaning among students and between students and teacher. This involves moving away from the traditional teacher-controlled IRE pattern (Cazden, 1988; Mehan, 1979). In its place are a variety of teaching methods and interactional discourse patterns that can lead to more exploratory talk and collaborative forms of learning for students. Rather than rely on the teacher as source for all knowledge, students are encouraged to use texts (books, films, art, poetry), other people (peers, family, other adults), and themselves as sources of knowledge. Opportunities to collaborate with peers in the classroom offer increased levels of participation and engagement. In one large-scale study of fifth-grade classrooms in the Chicago area, researchers found children's involvement to be highest when they were working cooperatively (Stodolsky, 1988).

As the teacher reduces her or his control of all learning activities and encourages small-group work, this turning over of some decision making is often accompanied by a greater range of choices for students. Horwitz (1979) concluded that children who are given activity choices seem to exhibit more positive self-concepts and are more creative than those in programs in which the activities are all directed by the teacher. Yet mere activity choice alone is certainly not sufficient to provide for what Edwards, D., and Mercer (1987) term a "handover of competence from teacher to child" (p. 91). However, as the authors carefully demonstrate in their book *Common Knowledge*, this handover is no simple feat. They note that it is the asymmetry of power between teacher and child that makes this handover so difficult. So again, the power relationship between teacher and students undergirds relationships of knowledge construction. For teachers who desire changing from transmission teaching to dialectical teaching, power and authority are central issues that are interwoven into classroom interactions.

OBVIOUS PROBLEMATICS

There is a desire in developing an analysis of shared authority to romanticize the project and declare that authority can actually be shared in hierarchical, institutional relations such as found in schooling. However, caution and skepticism must prevail because in classrooms (unless they've run completely amok—see McLaren, 1989) the teacher *is* ultimately in charge, responsible for student learning and classroom control. How much was actually turned over to students? Are there real opportunities for students to share authority for knowledge and process, or are there merely brief moments where students are just fulfilling the teacher's own agenda and thinking it is theirs? Is shared authority a utopian notion of autonomy and freedom?

Sharing Authority and Social Class

Valerie Walkerdine (1990) in her book *Schoolgirl Fictions* argues that holding out the freedom of progressive pedagogy to working-class children in our current society is offering them a false, imagined world that doesn't exist. In fact, she posits, progressive forms of pedagogy in which children are given choices and opportunities to construct their own understandings actually serve to enslave children, albeit in covert ways. As she writes:

> The forms of pedagogy necessary to the maintenance of order, the regulation of populations, demand a self-regulating individual and a notion of freedom as freedom from overt control. Yet such a notion of freedom is a sham. (p. 19)

Walkerdine goes on to critique forms of pedagogy in which the power of the teacher is denied as she assumes the role of benevolent helper/nurturer/mother.

This critical stance certainly means that to embrace notions of shared authority requires that classroom interactional data be analyzed in the context of the students' and school's location in the society at large. It is true that teachers who seek to share authority with students do so with the expectation that students will develop and expand their capacity to regulate themselves. This, after all, is the promise of education: that children will grow into autonomous adults. This autonomy is threatened, however, by social, political, and economic realities that restrict the access of the poor and many people of color to the culture of power (Delpit, 1988). Schooling, as a powerful institution in society, tends to perpetuate social and economic stratification (Anyon, 1980; Apple, 1982; Bourdieu, 1973; Bowles & Gintis, 1976; Willis, 1977), so an analysis of shared authority to promote autonomy must take into account student and school positionings within the society.

As described in Chapter 1, Jungman Elementary School educates children from families that are among the most marginalized in our country. The children in Room 104, then, have not had all of the economic, linguistic, and educational privileges that help smooth the passage into mainstream success. In many cases neither they nor their parents have had access to the dominant secondary discourses (Gee, 1987) connected with school. Schooling, then, has the potential to offer access to these powerful discourses in ways that have the potential to both liberate and subjugate.

Education alone cannot rectify the massive maldistribution of power, resources, and privilege we have in our country. As Walkerdine (1990) has noted, none of us are free, although some of us are more free than others; indeed, the gap between the relatively affluent 85% of U.S. society and the 15% who are desperately poor continues to widen (Richman, 1990). Schooling can, however, give students tools with which to confront the problems of fundamental social inequity. We can be conscious of the restrictions placed upon students by race, class, and gender oppressions in this society. And it is from a position of knowledge and consciousness that they will be able to act. It is imperative, then, that students be taught in ways that increase their ability to initiate, direct, plan, and execute classroom work. By learning early that they can speak and act with authority, they will be in a position to carry these important skills with them into their adult lives. There is, of course, an inherent danger in developing such skills: Is it wise to encourage urban, poor children to think and speak for themselves when they will enter a world in which critical thinking and outspokenness are labeled hostile and rebellious acts when coming from people who are not white or rich?

Obviously, educating students in classrooms where authority is shared will not end their social and economic oppressions. These students also must be able to read, write, calculate, research, speak, and think in ways that will help to give them entry to a culture of power (Delpit, 1988) that may be less than willing to admit them. Along with the knowledge that they sometimes have the power to act and initiate must also be knowledge of the standard forms used by those in gatekeeper positions in our society.

Students from middle-class and professional families are typically given opportunities in school to learn to make decisions and share some power, for it is good practice for the role they will be expected to play when they become adults (Anyon, 1980; Spring, 1991). Working-class and poor students, however, are more often prepared for working-class jobs in which *following* directions is more usual than giving them. So if teachers in urban classrooms with nonmainstream students step out of this mold and share authority with students, it is imperative that these same teachers work with parents and the school community to discuss the implications and ramifications of an alternative pedagogy. Students, too, must be prepared to understand the relationships of power and control that are operative in the world as it exists.

Sharing Authority and Teacher Education

Another problematic of shared authority in the classroom revolves around teachers' attitudes toward control and education. After all, many of those who become teachers have received schooling in which teacher authority is wielded, not shared. And since many teachers were successful students, why should they work to change the practice of schooling? First, teachers and preservice teachers must be given opportunities to experience first-hand the difference between collaborative and didactic learning. This is not as simple as merely asking people to get into cooperative groups: The very nature of teacher education must be changed to include meaningful learning tasks and problem posing on the part of the participants. Teachers must be supported and encouraged to try out forms of pedagogy that respect students' understandings and value students' expertise. This will happen best when teachers' own understandings and experiences are valued in teacher education.

Teachers who do try to make changes must be supported and encouraged; it is difficult to "teach against the grain" (Cochran-Smith, 1991) and challenge traditional forms of transmission teaching. Such change involves risk taking and serious intellectual work. As Anne related:

What I'm always doing is thinking, thinking, just thinking things through. Where have I come from? What am I doing? Where was I last year? Small groups scared me. Changing the desks scared me. There are times when it's still like rrrrrrrrr to me. When the noise level is too high and I think it's too loud for me. There are certain kids who mess around too much. I wonder. I guess you just have to watch. (6/10/92)

Teachers like Anne should not have to do their watching and their thinking alone. University educational researchers must work to share authority with teachers. We must make room for *teacher* initiations and expertise, both in defining research agendas and in interpreting classroom data. It is by working in relationships of co-agency between teachers and researchers that we can begin to address together the future of our world's classrooms. This is surely a mutual agenda, and one that should be co-constructed as we move closer and closer toward relationships in which teachers and researchers can initiate—both developing and sharing our mutual expertise.

3

"How Come We Haven't Done Any Work Today?"

Sharing Authority and Classroom Process

Teaching ought to open gates, not close them; people only begin to learn when they go beyond what they are taught and begin teaching themselves. This is teaching in my view: creating situations that impel people to reach beyond themselves, to act on their own initiatives.

—Maxine Greene, "Literacy for What?"

The first graders in Anne Barry's class were lined up at the door with the exhausted, disheveled look so common at the end of a busy school day. There had been the usual frenzy of finding and zipping coats, packing schoolbags with books borrowed from the class library, and rushing to get to the front of the line. Then there were some calm moments when all the students were ready to go and the bell hadn't yet rung. This conversation caught my interest:[1]

> MAYA: (Speaking to Anne) How come we haven't done any work today?
> ANNE: You think we haven't done any work today?
> MELINDA: Graphs. We did graphs.
> ANNE: Writing and reading about things that you like—isn't that what we do at school?
>
> (11/8/91)

After an extremely busy day, packed full of different learning activities, Maya questioned the teacher about the legitimacy of the day's school activities. As teachers embrace alternative pedagogies, what counts as a worthwhile learning activity often changes. Even though Maya was only in her second year of formal schooling, she knew that Anne's class was departing from the traditional format of

---

1. See Appendix B for transcription notation.

31

schooling. This chapter documents a typical school day (November 8, 1991) to provide the context for understanding the five routines that are described in more detail in the chapters that follow. By tracing the events of one school day, I also want to demonstrate the particular ways that students shared authority for directing classroom process. This sharing of authority had particular ramifications for Anne in regards to classroom management and decision making, and these issues are described in some detail. In addition, parents noticed that their children's first-grade experience was different both from their own and that of older children who had had Anne as a teacher in previous years; their reflections are included at the end of this chapter.

BEGINNING THE DAY

This school day in Room 104 began with the weekly physical education period taught by the PE teacher. Anne picked the class up at the gym and escorted them en masse to the water fountain located on the second floor. (It was a school rule that students go as a whole class to the bathroom and the water fountain.) The students filed back into the classroom and sat at their desks with detachable chairs set up in a traditional row format facing the chalkboard. Anne went to the front of the room, and the children began chanting "Twenty days until turkey day." Anne took up her position at the corner of the board, apparently signaling the beginning of an elaborate ritual of weather and calendar. Anne chose various volunteers for the next series of activities. Miriam came to the front to turn the hands on a weather wheel and describe the weather for the day. Silvia indicated the day of the week by picking the correct sentence strip that read "Today is Friday." Valentina went to the side of the room where a calendar of November was attached to a movable bulletin board and wrote the numeral for the day of the month. Montrel volunteered to move a huge paste-up of a thermometer to the correct temperature for what was predicted on the news. This all was completed within 20 minutes, and Anne signaled an activity change by taking out her journal and saying, "I'm going to get my journal and write what you liked from yesterday."

Journals

As Anne got her journal, children began raising their hands, telling her what they enjoyed. Five minutes later, she told them to get their own journals out. Her only direction was, "You can write about anything you like." This power to choose one's own topic has been granted to the students, as Anne indicated by her next statement, "I let you decide."

Everyone in the class was busy writing within seconds. There was some subvocalizing, some humming, and some shuffling of feet, but Anne did not look up from her own journal writing. The rule, although not stated at the outset, turns out to be, "No talking allowed," as two children started whispering and Anne gave them "The Look"—an intense, displeased stare with raised eyebrows. One inventive student, intent on borrowing an eraser, used gestures to arrange the loan and then, quite furtively, snuck a few rows over to grab it.

After about 10 minutes of quiet writing, Anne put down her journal and started moving around the room, conferencing with individual students about their writing. The students read their journal entries to her, and she wrote the conventional spelling of some words underneath their invented ones. Miriam got up from her desk and moved to the back of the room, settling down to read *In a Dark, Dark Wood* (Carter, 1991). Anne must have noticed this, since she immediately announced to the class, "If you're done and done with your picture, you may go back. No buddy reading today. Read by yourself for six minutes."

This transition from journal-writing time to book-reading time was initiated by a student who did not seek the teacher's permission to change activities. Anne, however, did not always allow students to move directly back to get books and read. Sometimes she said, "I want to see what you wrote" or "That was too fast, I want you to spend more time with your writing." As I spent more and more time in her classroom, I began to see the differential treatment of student initiations, based upon her beliefs regarding what steps the individual student should take next. The same behavior—putting the journal away and moving to the back of the room to pick a book—was differentially either negatively sanctioned or validated. In this particular case, Miriam's move from journal writing to book reading was validated by a specific direction from Anne regarding limiting the book reading to students who had finished writing and drawing. She further limited the book reading by proclaiming that students should do it alone today, rather than with a buddy.

In Miriam's move from journal writing to book reading, she can be seen as having found what Mary Manke (1990) calls the seams between and within classroom procedures. As she explains it:

> Teachers . . . can determine the amount of structure that will be built into the learning activities available in their classrooms. Highly structured activities function to limit the amount of interactional work that can take place, and therefore the opportunities that students have to contribute to power structures in classrooms. This is not to say however, that students do not find the seams in these environments and activities and use them to make their own contributions to power relationships. (pp. 241–242)

In this way, Miriam, in putting her journal away, getting up from her seat, and picking up *In a Dark, Dark Wood*, can be seen as seizing the initiative to direct classroom procedures—the process dimension of teacher authority. By Anne's inviting other children to join her ("If you're done, and done with your picture, you may go back . . . ") the teacher has not only validated Miriam's initiative but has also affirmed her own *authority* as being able to grant such permission to the rest of the class. Yet even in this reestablishment of teacher authority as director of classroom procedures, Anne turned over some of the decision-making regarding that change to the students: "If [*you* are] done," leaving it up to the individual student to determine *if* she or he is done—or at least if the student thinks the teacher would think she or he were done.

Class Schedule

This small exchange points to the curious dance of authority sharing in this classroom. A significant source of openings for initiations—seams, if you will—came from the flexibility of Anne's schedule. As required by her principal, Anne completed a time distribution for each day and week indicating how many minutes would be spent on each subject area. She rarely decided on the exact order of activities, nor how long each activity would last. For instance, on this particular day, she did not know in advance how much time students would spend reading and so had not announced to the class whether it would be buddy reading or individual reading. It was her idea that buddy reading takes more time to negotiate, so when she looked at the clock and saw it was almost time for lunch, *then* she made her announcement regarding the specific parameters of reading time for that day. Such schedule flexibility offered students *seams* to interject their own desires and plans into the process. It was almost a daily occurrence that a student would say, "We could do our journals now"—a particularly popular activity. By the last few months of school, these suggestions were taken up by students as specific invitations. By this I mean that on *many* occasions such a suggestion was immediately enacted without waiting for Anne's endorsement. So within literally seconds each student had her or his journal out and had started writing. As Anne describes it:

> I don't really have a set schedule. I know I'm going to do reading some time during the day, but it sort of evolves. They spend a lot of time every day writing [in their journals], and it's usually in the morning. At the beginning I really encouraged them to draw pictures, especially because it took me so long to get around to each one. Now that's not a problem because they can just go back and read. (3/30/92)

And then in May her routine of doing shared reading after journal writing had been relocated:

> I've been doing shared reading first thing in the morning while children are putting their coats away and collecting homework and getting organized. It

was just wasted time before. Also on days when I don't have preps [students go to art, music, and physical education] first thing in the morning I do something more focused on the board. (5/18/92)

So even within the flexible schedule can be seen *locations* of certain everyday routines: writing during the morning; shared reading initially segueing from journal time, and then later relocated to first thing in the morning; reading or writing teacher-led activities ("more focused activities") at the board first thing in the morning.

These decisions regarding placement of particular routines can be seen as Anne using her *classroom process authority* to determine certain fixed locations for regular activities. Yet planning for some flexibility regarding sequence and duration of activities allows students opportunities to have input regarding what they would like to do next. In many cases, such initiation of activities was suggested by a handful of outspoken youngsters: Maya, Montrel, Celina, and Claudio. Anne noticed this:

The stronger readers and writers are more of the initiators [of activities for the whole class]. I try not to let it happen that they're the only ones. I try to pull out from the others [what they want to do]. (5/4/92)

So even this brand of sharing authority—children suggesting the next class activity—can be seen as needing support from the teacher. This is the intriguing aspect of shared authority: An initiation that at first glance looks as if the teacher is being bypassed ("Let's do journals now"—and all the children take out their journals) presents an opportunity for the teacher to support other students in learning how to make such initiations. Thus the dilemmas and struggles of shared authority seem never to end: Even as Anne is sharing her authority over some classroom processes, she is thinking and planning how to encourage more initiations from quieter, less confident students. Therefore it can be seen that a teacher doesn't simply hand over control of classroom process, but rather carefully plots which pieces can be done by which students and considers who needs more support and involvement from the teacher. Even in the sharing of authority there is an assertion and a claiming of authority.

EARLY AFTERNOON

As the day continued, students filed back into the classroom from lunch. Anne turned off the fluorescent lights and asked, "What time is it?" A few children answered—without much enthusiasm—"Heads down." Most of the students crossed their arms and laid their heads down on their desks, but some plotting and scheming went on beyond Anne's sight. Apparently, my presence as another adult in the room didn't quite count in terms of getting caught: The whispers and the shared trinkets got passed only feet away from me. Obviously, I was not the one in authority here.

After five minutes, Anne announced, "When the light comes on, sit up, but don't take anything out of your desk." The latter part of the direction seems inserted to prevent excitement about unfinished journals or partially read books— taking them out might give them ideas and start a landslide that Anne doesn't want to deal with.

Teacher-Led Read-Alouds

Calling the students by rows, Anne gathered the children around her in the back of the room, sitting in a semicircle in the wooden and plastic chairs they brought with them. She started off with a clear expectation of who is supposed to talk: "Remember, this is *my* time to talk."

It was time for the teacher-led read-aloud. Anne had two books: *Fried Feathers for Thanksgiving* (Stevenson, 1986), a cartoon story about some witches, and *First Flight* (McPhail, 1987), a storybook with lots of informational content about a boy's airplane journey to visit his grandmother. These two books took 40 minutes to read, as a read-aloud in this classroom was almost never without students' diversion, conversation, and interruption. Although many teachers might consider such student diversions from her text to be going off on tangents, Anne had drastically changed her read-alouds that year, and fostering student talk during the read-aloud was part of her plan.

Plan might actually be too strong a word to describe what Anne actually had at the beginning of the year. More correctly, she had a question: What would happen if she used the read-alouds as a centerpiece of her reading instruction? How would the students and she talk about the books? What would be her role in discussing the texts? How would she manage it all?

Read-alouds used to be quiet affairs in which children sat quietly and listened to Anne read a book; now, however, read-alouds are loud, energetic affairs, with much talk among children and much movement in and out of seats. The reading of *Fried Feathers for Thanksgiving*, for example, was first interrupted when Camila matched the word *Thanksgiving* from the book with the same word from a poem on the nearby teacher-made bulletin board. Camila then began to read the poem out loud, and about half the class joined in. At the end of the poem Camila suggested, "A heart should go next to the word *care*." Anne replied, "Well, you'd like to make pictures to go with it. Let's do that, and we'll see in your pictures how you care." This was followed immediately by, "So who wants to go back to the book and see what happens?"

This diversion from the teacher-selected text to the poem was initiated by a student and allowed by the teacher. Anne was able to incorporate Camila's suggestion regarding the meaning of the word *care* and extend this initiation into an activity for the entire class. This, then, shows the special challenge for the teacher who is attempting a more collaborative style of teaching: not only honoring student initiations, but building on them—constantly expanding the possibilities for the group as well as for individuals within the group. So again, far from giving up power, the teacher who shares authority can be seen as *extending* authority as she or he utilizes the initiations and understandings of the students as a foundation for extending learning in directions that might not have been planned.

Camila can be seen as sharing Anne's authority for classroom process and content: For those minutes of the read-aloud time, Camila's interest in the Thanksgiving poem directed the attention and the work of the class. The student who initiates dictates how the other group members will spend their next few moments, especially if that initiation is taken up, or honored, by the teacher. In this case with Camila, Anne was excited by the print awareness Camila's initiation reflected. In fact, Anne used Camila's print awareness to expand the print awareness of the rest of the class. By following her initiation, Anne was validating Camila's knowledge—both the recognition of the word *Thanksgiving* and the understanding of the word *care*.

Yet even as Anne was able to recognize Camila's contributions, she still felt the responsibility to return to the read-aloud and finish the book: "So who wants to go back to the book and see what happens?" Other digressions occurred in the next half hour: a choral count by tens from 40 when someone notices the page number; a journal excerpt read by Valentina between books (Anne noticed she had brought her journal to the read-aloud despite the prior direction to get nothing out of the desk); a group chant of a finger play; and numerous discussions initiated by students regarding the content of the books.

Anne finished the read-aloud and denied Maya's suggestion that they do "Estimation" next. Anne informed the group that she would pick rows to line up for a bathroom break. Adrian suggested that she pick by colors of clothing, rather than by rows, and she not only took up his suggestion but put him in charge of naming the colors. Adrian then enlisted the help of Claudio, who had been giving him advice regarding color selection anyway.

Shared Reading

Back from the bathroom, Anne announced: "I'm going to let you have more time with the books and journals today." After giving some specific directions about journal writing, she went on to explain how the reading time would work, but then also added instructions regarding homework collection:

This is totally reading time. It's not counting time, or time to write on the chalkboard. It's time to get a book. The book you've picked is the one to read. Also, now is the time to put my books back. If you think you have my books, put them back now. Then get your homework out—that's another little job we haven't done. (11/8/91)

Claudio and Celina began collecting the homework, without cues from Anne. "Melinda, where's your homework?" asked Celina. Claudio went over to help Adrian look through his desk for his homework. Anne immediately began conferencing with Felipe on his journal, and Celina and Claudio finished collecting homework and put it on Anne's desk. At this point all the students in the room were busy writing or reading, and Celina and Claudio went to find books, too.

For the next 45 minutes, children read, moving in and out of small groups and pairs, as Anne continued to conference with individual students on their journal writings. At this point I was deluged by requests to "read with" individual students and turned my field notes into a sign-up sheet, becoming much more of a participant in the class than an observer. It turned out that "read with" meant different things to different students who signed up to read with me. To Henry it meant that I listened while he read out loud, while to Silvia it meant that I read to her. To Miriam and Melinda it meant that I listened while they read out loud together at the same time.

Shared reading is an activity in which students direct how they interact with books and with whom this interaction takes place. They utilize most areas of the classroom: individual desks still lined up in rows; chairs clustered around the kidney-shaped table near Anne's desk that is home to the collection of Big Books; desks lined together forming a long table in the back of the room, with books neatly fanned out covering themes of autumn and Thanksgiving; an area near the easel that, rather than being ready for painting, serves as a resting place for more Big Books and small versions of them; the area in the back of the room with a small collection of chairs that is used during read-alouds; and the most popular spot of all—the brown, swivel office chair on rollers used for author's chair. The one location I never saw a child sit for shared reading time was behind the teacher's desk, but I never saw Anne sit there either.

Shared reading is an activity in which sharing authority is embedded in the very structure of the routine as it was constructed by Anne and her students. Students choose where they want to be in the room, pick a partner or elect to read alone, select reading materials, and can also move among locations, partners, and materials without securing permission from the teacher. The very procedures of shared reading include a sharing of authority in the process dimension and have obvious spillover effects in the content dimension of authority as well. In fact, it was during shared reading that many students could be heard networking on topics of interest to them. It was common to hear one student approach another with a book in hand saying, "Here's the book you were looking for." So not only was the teacher sharing her authority with the students, but the students shared their knowledge with one another: They became experts on each other's interests.

Child-Led Read-Alouds

After a 20-minute, whole-group math activity called "Estimation," Anne announced, "Get into your groups." Children slid their desks and chairs into clusters of four and five; each group was designated by a number that Anne had given them, and there was a specified location for each group. This transition was smooth and without complaint, contestation, or discussion on this occasion. By spring, and with the arrival of five new students, there *was* active challenge over which group the student would join, as well as whether the student would join any group at all. In fact, I witnessed one occasion in which Celina—without negotiation with Anne—simply joined a group of her choice, rather than her assigned group. Anne never seemed to notice and nothing was ever said. The groups were carefully designed by Anne to balance by gender, reading proficiency, comfortableness with writing, and distribution of "talkers" among groups.

As the groups got settled, the class became involved in what I have come to call "child-led read-alouds." The formation of small groups was not needed for this whole-class activity, but Anne wanted them to be ready to shift into a small-group activity when attention to the student readers waned. An early version of this routine involved one student at a time reading her or his journal out loud to the class. The reader comes to the front of the room, after being chosen by the teacher, sits in the author's chair—which in this classroom is called "the everything chair"—reads a selection out loud, and gets a round of applause (usually initiated by Anne).

On this day Anne started by asking, "Felipe, would you like to share?" He shook his head no, to which she replied, "If your hand's not up, you really mean it, don't you?" In this sense, then, the invitation to read one's own writing to the class can be seen as an authentic invitation—the student is able to decline it. In this brief exchange over classroom process, Anne deferred to the author's authority. Pagano (1990), in writing about authority and teaching, states:

> "Authority" in all of its meanings refers to some sort of power or right. When teaching is considered to be an enactment of a narrative, "authority" refers to the power to represent reality, to signify, and to command compliance with ones' acts of signification. (p. 103)

In sharing authority, then, the teacher is actually sharing the power to represent reality. This is particularly apparent during journal sharing, where the narrative voices heard are those of children and the decision to share such a narrative is that of the author. The job, then, of the teacher in this forum becomes one of stage manager (deciding who will go on next) and coach (encouraging shyer students to participate).

At this early point of the school year, the only texts of child-led read-alouds were student writings. These included a variety of genres: poetry, jokes, letters, autobiographical narratives, and fictional stories. By February, though, child-led read-alouds had expanded to include students reading children's literature to the class. Students initiated this change by asking Anne repeatedly if they could read a particular book to the class. Many times the number of requests became a deluge, which meant that Anne had to sort through them to provide equal participation rights. She often urged students to "practice more" with a book before she would give them permission to read to the group.

THE DAY'S END

After a short round of "Show and Tell," Anne told the class they would have "Puzzle Time"—an activity done in small groups using a selection of puzzles and manipulative boxes from a special table near the door. Before she called on each group to go and select their puzzles, she gave this direction: "Anything you have of mine, pencils or crayons, put them back now, please." She turned to me and said: "Just that I'm doing this is very significant. I didn't used to do this. I would have one child walk around and collect them."

I probably wouldn't have thought twice about Anne's direction regarding the materials, except perhaps to note that she called the books and writing implements her own, rather than that of the class. Yet to Anne, this movement of children around the classroom—taking care of one of the basics of classroom procedures—was an important step. By permitting students to return materials, she was indicating a few things to them: She viewed them as knowledgeable regarding where her materials belonged; she saw them as capable of completing this task expeditiously; and she thought of them as honest regarding the ownership of materials.

SHARING AUTHORITY FOR CLASSROOM PROCESS

Moving now from an examination of one typical school day into a broader discussion of shared authority for classroom procedures, it should be noted that no teacher can ever control *all* classroom process, even if the teacher wants to and tries to. Even if the teacher maintains an iron grip and every student always follows each direction (a notion so impossible we don't even need to explore it), there are just too many movements in a classroom full of students in the course of a school day to ever possibly control them all. The sheer enormity of the control of classroom procedures, and hence teacher authority implicated in these processes, is a large part of what scares preservice teachers.

Negotiating Classroom Work

Certainly, in Room 104, there were many procedures *not* turned over to the students. For example, students were required to enter and exit their desks by walking in the back of the classroom—this was Anne's method of crowd control. Other crowd management techniques included waiting to go to the coatroom until the teacher called you and asking permission to sharpen your pencil. More generally, Anne established a non-negotiable authoritative stance in other ways as well: limiting the number of books that a child could take home each night to two; deciding which activities would be done in small groups, floating groups, or individually; deciding which activities would require raising hands and being called on to speak versus just jumping into the conversation.

The ways in which students challenged the teacher's authority, or pushed to discover where the seams were, were times that Anne characterizes as "bumps." These were moments when students were exercising their authority in ways that she did not like. They may have been clamoring to do something she did not want to do, getting excited and speaking among themselves and ignoring her directions, or not following classroom procedures she had set up for the orderly movement from one activity to the next. These "bumps," then, demonstrate how children's sharing of authority was not always a desirable notion for Anne as a teacher. Often the suggestions coming from the children would fly so fast and furiously she could not respond to them all. Mostly these were students' suggestions regarding activities or texts. The following excerpt illustrates how students negotiated with the teacher what their next work would be.

ANNE: I'm ready, put your books away now. Ready, set oookaaay. Marcos. When I went to my mailbox last night, there was a letter for us. The real mailman comes in and delivers mail to the school. You and I all together got a letter. I could hardly wait, so I opened it.

MAYA: What did it say?

CHILDREN: Who's it from?

HENRY: The jolly postman? [This is an intertextual comment (see Chapter 4) referencing the book *The Jolly Postman* (Ahlberg & Ahlberg, 1986).]

ANNE: A postman brought it. (Anne shows them the envelope and talks about the canceling and delivery process. She reads the address. Students interrupt her at the zipcode and recite: "60608." Students and Anne discuss why they have the same zipcode at home as at school.)

LOLA: Who's it from? (Anne is making a mystery out of it and the kids are guessing that it's from Mrs. Vargas [the former music teacher]. Anne reads the card and letter out loud without telling them whom it's from. The kids interrupt the reading to make guesses about whom it's from. Anne finishes reading the letter, including the signature from the former student teacher.)

ANNE: I'm going to leave it out.

CLAUDIO: Write her name on the board. Maybe we could write her a letter today.

CELINA: Could we write her a letter now?

ANNE: Okay. (Lots of kids talking all at once about what they can write in the letter and how they can draw pictures.)

ANNE: Ready, set. Okay, I like that much better. Miriam wanted to read to us today and I promised. I'm going to let you sit in the author's chair— the everything chair.

CLAUDIO: Want me to help you, Miriam? (Miriam nods yes, and Claudio comes up and stands beside her as she reads *Chicka Chicka Boom Boom* [Martin & Archambault, 1989].)

(3/6/92)

The suggestion made by Claudio for the students to write a letter got acted upon right after Miriam's read-aloud. Even though Anne agreed to Celina's request that they write their letters immediately, a few seconds later, she shifted abruptly away from the letters when she remembered her promise to Miriam. This excerpt shows the high level of student involvement in shaping the discourse of the classroom. In this brief exchange, students asked six questions regarding both process ("Could we write her a letter now?") and content ("What did it say?"). Claudio goes so far as to give the teacher a process direction: "Write her name on the board." Anne followed Claudio's direction and wrote the name on the board after Miriam had finished her read-aloud. Clearly, these students had many opportunities to share authority for shaping the work and talk of this classroom.

This, however, presents the teacher with the need to schedule all the work of the classroom, sometimes on a moment-to-moment basis. Rather than follow all students' initiations and suggestions, Anne had to decide whether to have the child-led read-aloud first, or the letter writing first. Another decision revolves around how much time to allot to one activity. As she said later in the day as the students were still writing their letters: "This is going well, but it's taking a long time. My frustration is deciding about spending this much time on it. But if I didn't, I'd fear losing momentum."

Therefore teachers who set up the work of their classrooms built around authentic purposes need to engage students in negotiating what this work will be. Additionally, since the talk in these classrooms offers openings for students to initiate, interrupt, and direct, the teacher must orchestrate the many suggestions and requests she or he receives in a day. This is no simple feat. In Anne's words:

I'm noticing . . . lately the new set of behaviors that I need to worry about. They were at different levels of shyness, but now! I never had to worry about this before. All I do is figure things out! It's driving me crazy! (12/16/91)

Although a very experienced teacher, Anne had a new set of things to figure out when she started encouraging and following student initiations. In all her years of teaching, she had never had to worry about what to do when children initiated; now students often participated so much that she said it drove her crazy.

Even as teachers attempt to honor student initiations, sharing authority for classroom process and content should not be seen as the *giving up of authority*. Rather, what is involved is a shift of how authority is maintained and expressed. Teachers use their authority to include students in the process of shaping classroom work and classroom talk. Teachers who share authority allow for students like Claudio to participate in directing not only his own but others' learning. It allows him to ask, "Do you want me to help you, Miriam?" thereby offering peer scaffolding and support for literacy tasks. The work of the students in the classroom, then, becomes work they have participated in shaping, both in form and in content.

Student Initiations and Classroom Control

Taking students' initiations seriously worked to encourage students to initiate with other teachers in the school. Although exciting to Anne as a teacher who wants to share her authority and encourage student initiative, it presented problems to her as well. She related the following event to the teachers' group:

Today the music teacher came in and taught them a song that happened to be in the *How I Wonder* book [a basal reader] that Camila loves so much. So she got up and went and got the book and showed it to the teacher and said, "See, it's right here." It didn't mean as much to the music teacher as it did to me, naturally. But I knew what Camila was going to show her, and I let her get up and get the book. I didn't say, "No, no, don't go over there." (6/1/92)

As evidenced in this narration, Anne felt a certain amount of conflict regarding what she might be creating that other teachers would have to deal with. "I let her get up," indicates that Anne contemplated *not* letting her get up and disrupt the music teacher's control and flow.

Anne also grew increasingly concerned about students' behavior when she wasn't with them. She heard repeatedly from other teachers in the school and from substitutes that they were hard to control. As Anne explained:

As soon as they see that I'm not here, it sets them off right away. That's an issue, it really is. Yesterday we were watching a video and they were into their second one—it was probably a little too much—Mrs. Clark came in and I was talking to her. In two seconds they were up like—somehow they think they can. And I said, "Don't you ever do that again." I was surprised they were so bold about it. (4/3/92)

So the very actions of self-initiation that Anne finds so exciting when related to literacy become problematic to her when the children are acting on their own in nonliteracy events.

Some days, she got frustrated and worried about what she should do to change her teaching and address the new problems she was discovering. Anne talked about this at length one day at lunch:

I have to figure out a few things. They couldn't do gym. It leads me back to the authority. Do they have too much initiations, and they can't take the responsibility? Maybe because I have to be very careful when I do certain activities that they understand now you may not talk, or when we talk you raise your hand. Other times you may talk and I don't care if you raise your hand. More parameters. But it wasn't a problem earlier, I could allow it to happen. Part of it is all the new kids. Guillermo is eight, and this is his second time in first grade. Then there's Veronica. I'm not sure how much she can read. She has no idea how to write. Wednesday was terrible; I threw whole language right out the window. I had them write, "I know how to behave," and said, "If you want a mean teacher, I will be a mean teacher. But you're not going to go to another class and treat another teacher that way." They could not go to [gym] and follow the directions there that they know. Mr. Lopez [the principal] saw how they were acting. They figured things out better before about what was expected of them. Now they seem to be testing it. I'm so frustrated with it. I'm up and then I'm down. It's driving me crazy. (4/10/92)

Anne recognized the connection between opening up her classroom to student initiations for both classroom process and knowledge and the behavior of her students when they were in other settings. This is an important consideration for teachers, particularly less experienced teachers, when they initiate radical changes of their teaching theory and methods. Stenhouse (1975) wrote about this concern based on classroom reform with teachers in England:

Any innovation at [the] classroom level must face the problem of control, and too many innovative proposals have given insufficient attention to this. But the problem does not stop there, for radical curriculum changes involve changes in the entire tone, code or ethos of the teacher–pupil relationship. (pp. 167–168)

Teachers who share their authority with students are in a constant process of negotiating and renegotiating their authority, as well as scaffolding students' success outside the classroom. It is clear, then, that classroom changes cannot be addressed in isolation of the wider school and home community. Thus sharing authority with students for classroom process and knowledge when *within* the teacher's agenda of becoming literate may create problems for the teacher when students become bold in other areas of school life as well. Anne realized that by opening the floor to student initiations for both knowledge and process, she also had to teach the students when to use this power. A year later, she reflected on what she'd learned:

This year I have a better idea of the connection between the knowledge and the process dimensions of authority. I understand more so that for places like the gym and when it's more opened up to them, I need to give them more cues ahead of time about what I expect. So that when they're out in the other arenas it helps to make the bumps less. Things are smoother because of my understanding better. (6/4/93)

I think what Anne was pointing to here makes an important distinction for teachers who fear opening up the curriculum to student interests and experience. They are many times afraid of losing control of classroom process. Yet as Anne realizes, a teacher can *structure* classroom and school experiences by providing students with clear directions and expectations. Providing parameters—as Anne calls them—does not preclude allowing student initiations into the classroom.

Assertive Discipline

Anne's techniques for classroom control also sometimes involved her use of a series of strategies she had learned when Jungman teachers received inservice education on Assertive Discipline (Canter & Canter, 1976) two years previously. A typical application of this approach occurred during small-group puzzle time. The students had chosen their materials and started working with them at their clusters of desks. There was a low hum in the room as some children were talking and working together. All of a sudden Adrian let out with a loud yelp. Anne told him to take "five minutes out" in a chair lined up on the back wall. He went with no explanation, questions, or arguments. Anne came over to explain to me that it bugs her when children disrupt that way. "He gets an immediate drop down, not a warning. That is something powerwise that is probably a personal, personal thing . . . I consider that very disruptive."

I had previously seen Anne use a "Ready–Set–Listen" prompt when she wanted the students to settle down. She used it frequently throughout the day, and the children earned a minute of free time if they were quiet by the word listen. But this was the first time I had seen her use a time-out chair and what she called a "drop down." On a few occasions, she wrote students' names on the board for an infraction and then added a check for the next one. After accumulating three checks, the student was given a "drop down" and ordered to time-out. I always wondered what happened if they received more checks after the drop down, but I never got to see this. The positive points accumulated through Ready–Set–Listen were used in good weather to go outside to the playground. The school had a policy against recess—as do many Chicago public schools—and the children considered going outside to play a real treat. As powerful an incentive as this playground time was, however, I did not observe Anne using the Ready–Set–Listen prompt much as the year progressed. It was a common strategy in the first four months of school and then was resurrected only in times of loud excitement.

Anne talked to me about her use of Assertive Discipline:

> I think teaching got harder, through the years, just how the children are and where they're coming from. When I started teaching we had 37, 38 kids in a classroom. And as I taught, the children became harder. Disciplinewise, managementwise—I think management is really the phrase. So two years ago I saw I was giving them more power when I started using Assertive Discipline. I think that a lot of it started for me there, in that I could give up a lot of my hostility and give them more by being assertive. (11/8/91)

Many educationists would say that a behavior-modification approach such as Assertive Discipline is inconsistent with holistic pedagogy such as whole language. In fact, throughout the year I was in Anne's room, I wondered if she would start to question her use of this externally oriented behavior-management approach. I never initiated such a discussion myself, however, perhaps due to my own unresolved contradictions from preservice teacher "training" in behavior modification.

So because of my own uneasiness, I never broached the subject of discipline systems. Instead I sat back and watched how Anne operated. The drop-down chair was used irregularly; in all of my 22 days of formal observation, I only saw the time-out chair in use three times. However, there were few other visible forms of consequences to notice. For instance, no child was ever sent into the hall, or to the office. Nor, for that matter, were there class meetings or discussions about behavior or relationships. Far and away the most common technique for discipline was Anne's use of what I termed to myself "The Look." Multiple times throughout most days, Anne would raise her eyebrows, lower her chin, and stare intensely at a child. This look seemed to be effective; I never once witnessed a child ignoring the message to stop what they were doing.

This description of Anne's strategies for discipline is offered as a backdrop to the larger issue related to shared authority. As can be seen from the above description, Anne did not actively attempt to share authority with students for classroom governance, discipline, or rules. She did, however, spend a fair amount of time thinking about the consequences of her pedagogy on issues of behavior. As behavior tends to be a significant concern for my preservice teachers after their first urban teaching experience, I think it important to acknowledge that urban schools tend to have teachers more concerned with control than their counterparts in the suburbs. Since whole language invites children to initiate and to talk, it is not surprising that more suburban teachers have embraced this pedagogy than have city teachers. If control of behavior is a major concern, the thought of children moving around the room without permission, talking without always being called on, and making suggestions for the next activity would not look too appealing.

PARENTS' REACTIONS

At the end of the year "Celebration of Learning," I was curious to talk to parents about their impressions of their children's school year. Anne had organized this afternoon event for parents and friends to hear the children read out loud a piece of their choice. Some children read their own writing, while others read published books. Everyone read something. All 10 parents in attendance agreed to be interviewed on tape during the refreshment time. Two even stayed after school to continue talking. The positive reactions of the parents interviewed does not indicate that other parents—or even these same parents in another setting—were so supportive of their children's classroom instruction.

Ricky's mother hobbled into the classroom; she has a muscle disease that makes walking painful. A very shy and quiet woman, she confessed after the interview that she dreads coming to school since she had such bad school experiences herself. She told me she forces herself to come to all events because she thinks it is best for her son. Mrs. Ortiz had attended Jungman school herself, over 30 years ago. She reflected on the changes:

> The biggest difference I see between Ricky's education this year and mine when I went to school here at Jungman is that he gets to learn about real things. When he comes home every day I ask him what he learned in school, and it's always about real things like plants and animals. When I was in school, we never read about real things, just like Dick and Jane. He talks about real ideas. (6/10/92)

This mother's comment illustrates well how important content selection is within the process of scaffolding students' expertise. It is not enough to consider only the process dimension of authority—students becoming experts—we must also examine *what* they are becoming experts about. Becoming knowledgeable about Dick and Jane did not excite Ricky's mother as much as his expertise about plants and animals—"real things."

This developing expertise was attributed by Miriam's mother to the emphasis from the teacher on creating real reasons to learn and becoming autonomous:

> It's nice to see that the way she's learning to read, she *wants* to know how to read. All the little ones [Miriam's siblings] are trying, too. My 3-year-old, because she has her reading it to her, when she's not around, she'll turn the pages and say the words. I was born in Chicago and came to Jungman. I see that the teachers now are more focused on the children as individuals. I like how she gave them each an individual chance to read what they can read and she let them pick it out. She encouraged them to do it on their own. (6/10/92)

Lola's mother made similar points regarding learning to write:

> My daughter is constantly writing. She has poems and stories that she's writing. She has books she's writing on her own. It started after she came here. Mrs. Barry started it in the classroom, and she said she wanted to do it at home, too. She liked writing, but more so after she started first grade. A lot of times she can read to me what she wrote, and I can't read a word of it. I did a lot of that when I was young, too. My mother tore up my writing like that, but I try to give her more freedom, so she'll like writing. It took me a long time to get over that. I told her it doesn't have to be perfect. I wasn't allowed that freedom; it was treated as a waste of paper. I make sure that they get at least 15 notebooks each year. (6/10/92)

Melinda's mother was able to compare Anne's class from two years previously (before Anne began her changes) when her older daughter was in the class. She also made the connection between Melinda's first-grade experience and her becoming a more outspoken, confident communicator at home:

> I always like to say that Melinda is a chain reader. We'll be coming to and from school, and she'll be reading one book, and she'll have two or three others on her lap. She can forget everything else, but she makes sure that when we leave the house she has books. Everyone makes fun of her bookbag, they go, "What do you have in there—rocks?" She has a little boy holding up the bookbag because it's that heavy. She found a new way to carry her bookbag—through the front. My main thing I've noticed is that to her, reading is fun, it's not a chore. That's the difference I see having one

daughter in this class the way it is now. (Turning to Anne) I didn't see you were too much into that then, I didn't really hear from Claudia about books. Melinda's confidence is so high. She wasn't as outspoken before. She was more to herself. Now, you ask her, "What do you think of this?" and she'll give you an honest opinion. It's helped me at home on a personal level because she reaches out to me more. Now it's in her mind that it's okay to say what she's thinking, it's not going to get her into trouble. (6/10/92)

Melinda's mother's connection between the classroom method and her daughter's willingness to develop and express her opinions brings back Maxine Greene's quote used at the beginning of the chapter that schooling should help students act on their own initiatives. These initiatives are ones that these parents value; they see their children developing as thinkers (Ricky's "real ideas"), writers (Lola's writing poems and stories at home), and readers (Melinda as a chain reader). Thus children's developing expertise, autonomy, and freedom to think, write, and read are extended past the classroom walls and into the home lives of students, even transforming the parent–child relationship.

4

"It Gots An Egg"

Children's Initiations During Teacher-Led Read-Alouds

At the center of Anne Barry's newly revised reading instruction were the daily teacher-led read-alouds. Anne read a great variety of books throughout the course of the year: information books, poetry, stories, comic books, chapter books, predictable books, Big Books, joke books, and picture books. She used this time to introduce children to information relevant to a particular thematic unit, acquaint them with story grammar and the various parts of a published book (title page, publisher information, dedication, table of contents, epilogue, and so forth), familiarize them with books they would then be able to pick up and read themselves, and reinforce concepts of print awareness as well as phonemic awareness.

TEACHER READ-ALOUDS

The teacher-led read-aloud is a familiar routine, particularly in primary classrooms. Anne had always read out loud to her students in her previous 20 years of teaching. However, the *way* she read out loud and the *reasons* she read out loud changed dramatically. Anne used to read out loud no more than once a day, usually after lunch or recess as a way to calm the students down. They stayed at their individual desks, set up in rows as she stood at the front of the room and read the book without interruption. She thought that if they were quiet they were listening.

However, now Anne's read-aloud routine is changed in physical, cognitive, and social ways: Children gather around her in a semicircle in the back of the room, usually in their chairs, but sometimes on the floor; they make comments throughout the reading of most books; they talk to one another about the text without being negatively sanctioned by the teacher. This brand of read-aloud—what Anne and I call "interactive read-alouds" (Oyler & Barry, 1993)—is different from many classrooms in the extensive quantity of student talk permitted and, indeed, encouraged.

Studies on teachers' varying styles of talking and questioning during read-alouds have shown the impact of the teacher's discourse on students' responses and/or comprehension (Dickinson & Keebler, 1989; Dunning & Mason, 1984; Martinez & Teale, 1993; Peterman, Dunning, & Mason, 1985; Teale, Martinez,

& Glass, 1989). Yet little analysis has been done on read-alouds in which students have more control over questions and discourse. Nikola-Lisa (1992) recorded primary students' spontaneous talk during small-group sessions with picture books. In analyzing children's language and dramatic play around books, he argues that, "The 'text' young children generate in response to literacy events is never a digression, but an essential part of the meaning-making, symbol generating process indicative of human life" (p. 211). Thus the texts students generated during read-aloud discussion, and the teacher's responses to these texts, are the focus of this chapter.

Students' spontaneous comments during read-alouds in Room 104 captured my interest from the very beginning of this study. I viewed these student initiations—or spontaneous comments—as prominent markers of shared authority. Therefore, from the very beginning of my classroom visits, read-alouds were recorded on audiotape during each visit to the classroom. Additional information not able to be captured on audiotape was recorded in field notes.

STUDENT INITIATIONS

In this chapter, I examine the types of initiations students made during teacher-led read-alouds and the ramifications these initiations had for teacher authority. Students' initiating talk about texts is significant in both the process and content dimensions of authority. In the process dimension, students participated in shaping who talked, when they talked, and what was talked about; in addition, they often helped decide which book was read. Student initiations, then, can be seen as molding the discourse in the classroom. As Wood and Wood (1988) noted in their study of classroom questioning, students don't usually ask the questions in the classroom because whoever asks questions is dictating how the listeners will spend their "next few cognitive moments as well as what they will say" (p. 284). Thus, when students do get to ask questions and make comments, they can be seen as playing a large role in directing the work of the classroom.

It is clear from examining the talk that occurred during teacher-led read-alouds that students were sharing authority for many of the processes involved in the read-alouds. These initiations for classroom process had a direct effect on the content dimension of classroom authority as well. Remembering that the content dimension of authority refers to knowledge construction, excerpts from the read-aloud transcriptions demonstrate how information was shared, knowledge constructed, and expertise developed by children in their talk about books.

As Anne and I reviewed the transcripts, we noticed that the typical IRE pattern of teacher-controlled discourse had been displaced. What we realized is that student initiation had assumed an important place in shaping what was talked about during these teacher-led read-alouds. We began to examine the types of initiations the students made and identified seven different kinds. These are listed with brief descriptions in Table 4.1 (this is a revision of categories Anne and I derived together; see Oyler & Barry, 1992). Each type of student initiation is examined in detail through selected excerpts from various read-alouds.

Directing Process and Reading Text

The first excerpt includes two types of initiations—directing the process and reading the text:

(Children are gathered around Anne in their chairs. She has *Chickens Aren't the Only Ones* [Heller, 1981].)

(1)   ANNE: You know what? We have another chicken story. Let's see how we do.

(2)   CHILD 1: Paaack, paaack, paaack

(3)   ANNE: (Valentina is playing with a plastic toy.) Valentina, right now go take it and put it on my desk. Real quick so you don't miss any of this . . . Let's do this: ten little soldiers . . . (The class and Anne do a word and finger play and then Valentina comes back to the group.) The author is Ruth Heller.

(4)   CLAUDIO: (To Anne) Open it like this. (His hands are palms up with pinky fingers lined up and touching—making an open book symbol. Anne does not follow his direction.)

(5)   MONTREL: Open it like that. (He does the same hand motion as Claudio.)

(6)   ANNE: I understand what you mean now. (Anne opens the book, showing the front and back cover.) To see if there's something on the back. They wanna check out/

(7)   CHILD 2: It gots an egg. It gots an egg right there!

(8)   ANNE: Maybe you can see if there're other books that author wrote, or to see if the title page went from here to here. We've discovered that this year, haven't we?

(4/3/92)

One aspect that is not reflected in these transcriptions is the excitement that surrounded most of the read-alouds. Anne built on this enthusiasm, in large part by frequent comments reinforcing the students' growing knowledge about books. As can be seen from this passage, students had expertise that the teacher didn't. Their active participation resulted in a real exchange of information from students to teacher. In turns 4 through 8, Claudio and Montrel have noticed something about

TABLE 4.1. Children's Initiations During Teacher-Led Read-Alouds

Initiation Type	Description
Directing process	Gives teacher directions about the process of reading out loud: how to hold book, when to turn pages, what to read, when to start or stop
Reading text	"Reads" the text: pointing out words, pictures, phonemic patterns, chanting refrains
Questioning for under-standing	Asks a question to clarify understanding of picture, text, vocabulary, topic, or concept
Personal experience	Relates personal story, either real or invented
Intertextual link	References other texts: books, movies, songs, authors, illustrators, chants, poems, and so forth
Claiming expertise	Offers content knowledge from outside the text, not referenced by personal story or other text
Affective response	Relates a personal feeling evoked by text

the cover of the book: It has a picture that extends from front to back. In turn 4, Claudio begins *directing the process* of the read aloud (see Table 4.1). Montrel (turn 5) responds directly to this peer initiative, repeating Claudio almost verbatim. As Anne responds to this student initiation by following the children's direction and showing the entire cover to the audience, another student notices the significance of Claudio's initial direction and describes the picture in a way that neither Claudio nor Montrel did. Thus turn 7 is another type of student initiation—*reading the text*. In this example, reading the text refers to the student interpreting the picture ("It gots an egg. It gots an egg right there!"), but other ways to read the text include reading the words as the teacher reads them (or instead of the teacher reading them), making plays on words, chanting refrains in predictable books, or pointing out phonemic patterns. These were all common ways in which the students participated in reading the book, changing a teacher-controlled read-aloud to an interactive read-aloud.

A large part of the participatory nature of this read-aloud hinges on a sharing of authority that occurs between and among teacher and students. This sharing is enacted in both process and content dimensions. In the above excerpt, students' directions regarding what the teacher should do were followed by her, and then another student helped highlight the significance of this act by pointing out what to look at on the cover. Children here are getting opportunities to direct their own and one another's attention and, therefore, learning. It is important to see that these students were able to contribute something the teacher had not even noticed. This demonstrates how teachers can be co-learners with students, sometimes following their lead. That is, of course, a different kind of dialogue—typical of what Robert Young (1992) calls the "discourse classroom" as opposed to the "method classroom." In the discourse classroom, learners are partners with teachers, rather than objects, and pedagogy is co-constructed.

And yet, even as the teacher follows the students' lead in holding the book as directed, and students focus their attention on what other children have directed them toward, the teacher's job is not done: she then *extends* this attention (turn 8). Anne not only validates the students' initiations, but she adds to this knowledge by talking about other information a reader can find on the back cover besides a picture ("You can see if there're other books that author wrote"). She then gives the children credit for this discovery ("We've discovered that this year")—making metacognitive the process of learning and thereby empowering the learners.

Questioning for Understanding

Other types of student initiations can be seen as the read-aloud continues, but I will focus next on questioning for understanding.

(18) ANNE: OK, we're all set.
(19) CHILD: I hope we begin.
(20) ANNE: CHICKENS LAY THE EGGS YOU BUY. THE EGGS YOU BOIL OR FRY OR . .
(21) CHILD 2: Oil
(22) ANNE: DYE
(23) CLAUDIO: They die like that?
(24) ANNE: OR LEAVE ALONE SO YOU CAN SEE WHAT GREW INSIDE NATURALLY
(25) CHILD 3: Eggs
(26) MONTREL: A real baby chick. Baby birds are called chicks.
(27) GUILLERMO: Does that really happen?
(28) MONTREL: Yeah, that really happens. Cause I had a little bird, and he laid a egg, and then it opened.

(4/3/92)

In turn 23 Claudio is *questioning his understanding* of the text around confusion with *dye* for *die*. (This gets cleared up in a later discussion of the picture of dyed Easter eggs.) So, too, Guillermo poses a question in turn 27 regarding his understanding of the text ("Does that really happen?"). These questions children spontaneously ask throughout read-alouds are authentic questions: questions asked because they want to know the answer. In this way questioning by children does not fit into the common IRE structure. In the IRE pattern, teachers ask most of the questions. As mentioned in Chapter 2, these teacher questions, sometimes called pseudo-questions (Barnes, 1990), display questions (Hammersley, 1977), test questions (Getzels, 1975), or "guess what I'm thinking questions" (Postman & Weingartner, 1969), are designed to check student comprehension. In this type of exchange, then, the teacher is the expert and is checking to see if students are correct. Expertise, then, is all-or-nothing: The teacher has it, and the children do not. This type of questioning pattern can serve to restrict development. As Stubbs (1976) explains, there are cognitive benefits to such student-initiated questions:

> Children's language often becomes more complex and effective when they have to deal with real communicative tasks. . . . A child will be unable to display his [sic] total verbal competence if he is restricted to a passive response role, sandwiched between the teacher's initiation and feedback. The child must also have the opportunity to initiate discussion. It is therefore clear that if the status relations between adult and child are highly asymmetrical, the child's language will characteristically be much less complex than in conversation with social equals. (pp. 91–92)

Although in this dialogue the teacher and students could not be considered social equals—Anne is always the teacher—she steps aside for a few moments and allows Montrel to explain to Guillermo that birds do indeed hatch from eggs. So even in a teacher-led read-aloud, there can be time for social equals to talk in elaborated ways directly with one another.

An important benefit to the teacher willing to open the floor to children's questions is that such a teacher gets access to children's understandings. In the above exchange, for example, Anne found out that Claudio did not discern the difference between *dye* and *die* and that Guillermo was unfamiliar with the process of eggs hatching. These comments and questions, then, provided Anne with assessment information regarding the meaning her students were making of the text. This is particularly important in classrooms, such as Anne's, in which many of the children do not speak the language of instruction at home. Claudio's mother told me that they work very hard to maintain a predominantly Spanish-speaking environment at home, even teaching Claudio to read in Spanish. Thus vocabulary development in English occurs a great deal through literacy activities in school.

Students asked a variety of types of questions over the course of the school year during teacher-led read-alouds. Some had to do with the process of the read-aloud itself: "Can you read more Mrs. Barry?" or "Can you read my book next?" But the questions I want to focus on in this category of *questioning for understanding* deal with the *content* of the books. Children asked questions of the teacher and of one another for a variety of reasons: to learn or clarify meanings of words ("What are quilts?"), to distinguish fact from fiction ("Does that really happen?"), to explore reasons and interpretations ("How come it smells?"), and to check understandings ("She has a sister?").

In analyzing questions asked by students and teacher during read-alouds over the course of the school year, it is apparent that students' questions often sparked cross-discussion (Lemke, 1990) in which peers spoke directly to one another (see turns 26–28). Anne's questions, on the other hand, tended more to be aimed at clarifying students' understandings of the story line and did not usually promote multiple exchanges such as those seen in the egg dialogue.

Personal Experience

The fourth type of student initiation during read-alouds was quite common: Students offered their narrative of *personal experience* on a regular basis. Many times, these experiences were inserted as a way to substantiate a claim to knowledge. This is clearly visible in turns 27–28 when Montrel affirms to Guillermo that birds really do hatch from eggs: "Cause I had a little bird, and he laid a egg, and then it opened." Sometimes the personal experiences related by students included understandings that Anne challenged. In the transcript that follows (from another part of the same read-aloud), Celina is responding to an illustration of dinosaurs hatching from eggs. She tells about seeing dinosaurs at the zoo.

> CELINA: One time when me and my friend went to the zoo, I seen one of
>   those and I got scared/
> ANNE: Well, maybe it was/
> CELINA: Cause it was coming towards/
> ANNE: Are dinosaurs alive?
> MONTREL: No, they're dead meat.
> CELINA: It was laying down.
> CHILD 1: They're dead.
> CELINA: It was like this. (She curls on her side.)
> ANNE: Maybe you saw the skeleton. There's one that lays down in the Field
>   Museum.
>
> (4/3/92)

In this exchange Anne is sharing her authority and allowing the children to speak as experts by sharing their personal experience. At the same time, she is monitoring this expertise and using her knowledge as a more expert member of the community to bring the children's understandings and interpretations in line with the wider sociocultural community. As Jerome Bruner (1986) wrote:

> Most learning in most settings is a communal activity, a sharing of the culture. It is not just that the child must make his [sic] knowledge his own, but that he must make it his own in a community of those who share his sense of belonging to a culture. (p. 127)

This, then, is the job of the teacher who seeks to collaboratively construct knowledge with students: helping mediate the students' understandings in light of the teacher's knowledge of the larger culture. Anne knows that Celina did not see a dinosaur coming toward her at the zoo. But there is a gentle connection Anne urges to other cultural knowledge: There is a dinosaur skeleton at the Museum of Natural History, and maybe Celina is thinking of that one.

Students' personal experience stories represent one of the most challenging forms of claiming knowledge for teachers to deal with. At my urging, many of the preservice teachers in my classes employ instructional techniques that open the classroom conversational floor to students' knowledge, experiences, beliefs, and values. They frequently report that when children offer seemingly implausible information (like dinosaurs coming after them at the zoo) they don't know what to say. They worry about hurting the children's feelings or embarrassing them in front of their peers. They struggle against domination of teacher knowledge over student knowledge ("I know that what you said can't be true"). Yet as teachers we are responsible that students' misconceptions get corrected. Anne's ability to salvage Celina's story as a legitimate personal experience knowledge claim about dinosaurs is thus a graceful linkage acknowledging Celina's ability and right to bring herself into the read-aloud. It reminds me somewhat of the technique I learned while I was an aide in a preschool: The child comes up to you with a drawing of a rectangle and says, "Look at my triangle." The teacher answers: "It's a shape and a triangle's a shape; it has sides and a triangle has sides; if it has three sides it's called a triangle, and this one has four so we call it a rectangle." There is much room when responding to students to link their experiences to the knowledge in the wider culture.

There are times that the sharing of personal experiences did not continue the authoritative topic line of the text or teacher. In other words, the teacher was not rigidly binding student initiations to the authority of the text, or indeed to her own interpretations of what fit with the text at hand. As McCollum (1989) noted in her portrayal of one Puerto Rican teacher's more conversational (rather than recitation) style, the incorporation of divergent student-initiated topics into the discourse allows students who may not have the "correct academic information" (p. 150) to participate and succeed. This also has direct bearing on shared authority in the classroom, for, as Christie (1989) has noted, "whoever controls the textual theme holds the power" (p. 177). By students sharing their understandings of the book and not being bound to the textual theme as decreed by the teacher, the children are able to share authority for directing and constructing the knowledge of the classroom. In the next excerpt—from the read-aloud of *The Tree* (De Bourgoing, 1991)—Miriam adds her personal experience with seeds to the topic of how trees grow.

(1)   ANNE: A CHESTNUT IS A SEED OF A CHESTNUT TREE. A TREE IS A GIANT PLANT.
FOOD STORED INSIDE THE SEED NOURISHES THE YOUNG PLANT. AS THE
CHESTNUT SAPLING GROWS UP THE ROOTS GROW DOWN INTO THE SOIL/

[Turns 2–5 edited out]

(6) ANNE: Miriam. (Miriam is raising her hand.) Montrel, honey [asking
       him to stop talking]. Miriam.
(7) MIRIAM: In my backyard we have a little garden and we're growing
       seeds.
(8) ANNE: What are you growing?
(9) MIRIAM: Watermelon and corn and tomatoes.

                                                                    (4/10/92)

Miriam's personal connection to the topic of seeds was evidenced in her account of her backyard garden. Rather than sanctioned, bound off, or ignored
(McCollum, 1989), the teacher responded to the student's initiative with a question that encouraged her to elaborate. Thus the personal experience served to
connect and extend (Hynds, 1994) the textual information. Quite often, one
student's personal experience served as a spark for another's, as can be seen as
the above dialogue continues:

(10) ANNE: Angel. (He is raising his hand.)
(11) ADRIAN: We're planting a apple tree.
(12) ANNE: Are you planting an apple tree, too? Wonderful.
(13) TERRA: I don't have a garden.

                                                                    (4/10/92)

As this very long read-aloud unfolded, children related experiences with home
gardens, edible seeds, and caterpillars they had observed throughout metamorphosis. These topics were not the theme of the text, but they allowed the students
to connect their own experiences with the information presented in the text.

As the year progressed, the personal experiences the students related were more
and more frequently group experiences of the class as a whole. An example of
this is Angel's comment (turn 11, below) during the read-aloud of *A Walk by the
Seashore* (Arnold, 1990). Montrel has just gone to retrieve a comparison chart in
The Book of Animal Records (Drew, 1987), and Anne is reading the page Montrel
wants the class to see:

(1) ANNE: HE [a whale] WEIGHS MORE THAN 30 AFRICAN ELEPHANTS.
(2) CHILD 1: He's bigger than anything.
(3) MAYA: He's bigger than a house.
(4) SILVIA: I was going to say that.
(5) GUILLERMO: The whales don't eat nobody; he saves everybody.
(6) ANNE: Sit. And how many inches is a human?
(7) CLAUDIO: Mrs. Barry, the Sears Tower is bigger than anything.

(8) MARCOS: The sky's not bigger.
(9) LOLA: The sky's way, way up.
(10) ANNE: Let's see how much an elephant weighs so we can compare it.
(11) ADRIAN: Remember the dolphin show? The dolphin was standing on its tail, was walking on its tail.
(12) CHILDREN: Oh, yeah. (Lots of talk all at once about dolphin show)
(13) ANNE: The dolphins are in the whale family.

(6/5/92)

In this long discourse excerpt, Adrian (in turn 11) initiates a personal experience that seems to take the discussion even further afield from the topic of whales. The class had moved from a walk along the seashore, to whales, to the size of the Sear's Tower, to the sky. Anne made a bid (turn 10) to return to the book at hand. This was not taken up by the children, and Adrian initiated a new topic about the dolphin show the class had seen two months before. Adrian's personal experience is an example of narratives that were related by individual children of whole-class experiences. These group experiences demonstrate the growing body of common knowledge in the classroom community (Edwards, D., & Mercer, 1987). The teacher then seized upon this common knowledge to share expertise of her own (turn 13), thereby returning the conversation to the original topic of whales. Thus the sharing by students of personal/group experiences allowed the teacher to use her authority (of the content) to return the class back to the book at hand.

Intertextual Link

The above transcript excerpt was sparked by Montrel's intertextual link between the books *A Walk by the Seashore* and *The Book of Animal Records*. This type of intertextual initiation was frequent during all read-alouds but occurred most commonly during the reading of information books. In this type of initiation, students juxtaposed two texts: other books, songs, movies, filmstrips, poems, chants, and unpublished writings of their own. Sometimes the proposed intertextual link was not immediately obvious to the teacher, as in the following excerpt from the read-aloud of the book *Fiesta* (Behrns, 1978):

(1) ANNE: WE EVEN DIG FOR MEXICAN ARCHEOLOGICAL/ They bury things just like if you'd be on an archeological dig.
(2) CLAUDIO: Like Captain Hook.
(3) ANNE: Like . . . Captain Hook? . . Oh, buried treasure. Oh, I was thinking of Indiana Jones too.
(4) CHILD 2: I got that movie, Mrs. Barry.

(5/5/92)

It took Anne a few seconds to understand Claudio's intertextual link between buried treasure and Captain Hook (turn 2), but then she went on to propose an intertextual connection of her own (turn 3), one that was recognized by another student. This negotiation and acknowledgment of intertextuality brings to mind Bloome and Egan-Robertson's (1992) analysis that not only must the juxtaposition of two texts be proposed, but that it also must be "recognized, acknowledged and have social significance" (p. 12). Thus the teacher plays a powerful role in both recognizing and acknowledging intertextuality, but as is evidenced in turn 4, students can share this authority also.

Most frequently, intertextual links were made to other books and students would quickly leave the read-aloud semicircle to retrieve the text they remembered. Some students negotiated permission to do this from the teacher, but the most avid intertextual retriever (Montrel) never felt this need. This was a classroom contribution he took upon himself—one for which he received consistent teacher validation, as can be seen in the next excerpt during the reading of *Monarch Butterflies* (Gibbons, 1989).

(1)   ANNE: THE CATERPILLAR EATS AND GROWS AND BEGINS TO CHANGE. IT
            BREAKS OUT OF ITS OLD SKIN AND SHOWS NEW SKIN UNDERNEATH. THIS IS
            CALLED MOLTING. Molting.

(2)   MONTREL: There's a book about that. It's in *Creature Features* on the
            last page.

(3)   ANNE: On the last page? (Montrel goes and brings the book, opening
            to the last page.)

(4)   ANNE: No, that's not the one. Oh, there you go.

(5)   MONTREL: Oh, yeah, I see it. There it is.

(6)   ANNE: Wanna read the description of it?

(7)   MONTREL: (Reads text)

(8)   ANNE: Thank you, Montrel, for checking that out for us. Does that
            caterpillar match the one in this book?

                                                                          (5/20/91)

This teacher validation for Montrel's sharing of his intertextual connection demonstrates the important role students' intertextual links played in facilitating a sharing of authority during read-alouds. Not only does Anne allow Montrel's intertextual knowledge into the discourse of the classroom, but she deepens it by having him read the passage to the class. In her public thanks to Montrel for his intertextual initiation, Anne noted the role this student was playing in "checking out"—or authorizing—the information for the entire class. She then furthered this understanding by asking the questions that could be answered when comparing two texts: Do they match? In what ways are they the same, in what ways are they different? This stance toward a critical literacy—the reader can compare texts and generate interpretations—is a fundamental aspect of shared authority. That is, the text itself is not the ultimate authority: It is what the reader does with the text that counts. Montrel, then, is speaking and acting with authority in this classroom literacy event: He knows what book to retrieve from the shelf, he is able to find the page that applies, and he is encouraged to validate (or authorize) the information for the whole class.

Intertextuality is a negotiated process and thus a prominent marker for examining teacher authority. As Bloome and Egan-Robertson (1992) explain:

> No text—either conversational or written—exists in isolation, it exists in relation to previous and forthcoming texts. But which texts are and will be related is not a given. . . . People, interacting with each other, construct intertextual relationships by the ways they act and react to each other. (p. 7)

In the next two excerpts Anne can be seen acting and reacting very differently to two students' intertextual connections. The first excerpt records the continuation of the reading of *Chickens Aren't the Only Ones* (Heller, 1981). The text by this time is covering all different kinds of animals that lay eggs.

(142) ANNE: All right, hands down now, I'm going to keep going.
(143) CHILD 1: Yep.
(144) ANNE: FROG AND TOAD AND SALAMANDERS/
(145) CHILD 2: Frog and Toad All Together.
(146) MONTREL: We have that book over there.
(147) SILVIA: We got it right there. Teacher, *Frog and Toad Together*.
         (Dashes over to bookshelf with other children and gets books.)
(148) CELINA: Yeah, *Frog and Toad Are Friends*!
(149) ANNE: That's right (laughing).
(150) MONTREL: *Frog and Toad Together* and *Frog and Toad Are Friends*.
(151) ANNE: Yesss! This is unbelievable. You want to show her? Maybe
         some people haven't discovered that book yet. Yeah, ohhh.
(152) CHILDREN: *Frog and Toad Are Friends*.
(153) ANNE: You know what, I'm going to go to my favorite bookstore
         tonight, and I'm going to look up some more of those.
(154) MONTREL: I want to go to that bookstore.

The words in the information book being read out loud reminded a child (turn 145) of a title of a favorite series of fictional books about a frog and a toad who have adventures together (see Lobel, 1970, 1971). As these were easy-to-read favorites of most students in the class, the simple mentioning of the titles sparked much shouting. A few students dashed over to one of the bookshelves and found the Frog and Toad books, which they brought back to show the group. Rather than view this connection to other books as a distracting diversion, Anne used the opportunity to build on the students' enthusiasm about the book. Implicit in her message of going to her favorite bookstore (turn 153) is that her students' intertextual knowledge is valued, as is their interest in books. She extends their knowledge and excitement about Frog and Toad books by promising to supply even more of them for the classroom's library. It is important to keep in mind here that there are no bookstores in the Pilsen neighborhood. A few children brought in books from home over the course of the school year; they were, with the exception of Claudio's collection of classics, all "Golden Books" available in the local supermarket. (I should also note that teachers and parents who tried to purchase children's books in Spanish had an even harder time finding anything. Some of the bilingual teachers at Jungman finally resorted to ordering books from Mexico and Spain.)

In the above transcript, Anne not only acknowledges the intertextual link, expertise, and initiation of the children, but she follows it as well by permitting students to get the Frog and Toad books and promising to purchase more in the series. Anne did not always follow the initiations of her students, however. In the following excerpt from a different read-aloud, Anne treats the intertextual link as a distraction and uses her authority to "contest the legitimacy of the intertextuality" (Bloome & Egan-Robertson, 1992, p. 10). In this transcript, the teacher is reading from *The Gingerbread Man* (Parkes & Smith, 1984):

ANNE: DON'T WORRY HE SAID, I'LL CARRY YOU OVER THE RIVER.
CHILD 1: Over the river
CELINA: (Singing) Over the river and through the woods (other children join in singing) to grandmother's house we go/
ANNE: Does that go with the story?
CELINA: The horse knows the way to carry the sleigh
CHILDREN: No
ANNE: How about, you wanna sing that later?
CHILDREN: Yes
ANNE: OK. It reminded you—river. Let's sing that song later, we're almost done, ready?

(11/25/91)

In this case, Celina's intertextual link—juxtaposing the words from *The Gingerbread Man* with the Thanksgiving song that the class had learned—was not greeted with enthusiasm and excitement by the teacher; Anne contested the legitimacy of Celina's intertextual link. This, then, illustrates the powerful role of the teacher to either *legitimate* or *contest* intertextual links. This passage reflects very well that in making intertextual links, "entitlement rights are not distributed uniformly or equitably" (Bloome & Egan-Robertson, 1992, p. 10).

Do the book titles from fictional Frog and Toad adventures "go with" an information book about oviparous animals any more than a song with the same words "goes with" a retold story? I think not. For reasons that I do not know (time, fatigue, lack of interest, control), Anne did not want to follow Celina's intertextual initiation, whereas she did follow up the reference to Frog and Toad by allowing the students to go to the bookshelf and collect the books. An important detail to notice, however, is that even in Anne's dismissal of Celina's right to make the link, she acknowledged its source and authenticity. Even as she declared it did not belong in this read-aloud, she validated Celina's intertextual connection. Further, Anne offered the class the opportunity to "sing it later," which they indeed did; Celina made certain to remind her when the read-aloud was over.

As the year progressed, the frequency and sophistication of the students' intertextual comments grew. This reflects the growing body of common knowledge (Edwards, D., & Mercer, 1987) shared by this literacy community as well as the teacher's acceptance of such initiations. Even though the intertextual links, or for that matter any other type of student initiation, were not always followed and taken up, they were at least validated and legitimated.

Claiming Expertise

A sixth type of student initiation during read-alouds we have termed *claiming expertise*. These are student initiations in which they directly shared their knowledge from *outside* the text, without referencing personal experience or another text. These initiations were usually delivered with an air of authority and did not often sound like tentative, exploratory talk (Barnes, 1990). For example, Anne has just explained about how a "poke-and-look book" works and is showing the class *Look Inside the Earth* (Ingoglia, 1991).

(1) ANNE: You see the spiral binding allows the reader to turn the pages back like you shouldn't do with a regular binding.
(2) ADRIAN: That's like a spiral notebook. But it's a book, not a notebook.
(3) MONTREL: You can't write in a book like a notebook or you'd be in biiiiiiig trouble.
(4) ANNE: You're right. Okay, should we start?

(5/29/92)

Adrian points out the similarity of the spiral binding to that of the spiral notebooks that the students used for their daily journals, and Montrel contributes his understanding of the difference between these two items. Anne acknowledges this expertise of her students and signals her intention to start the reading. But by posing it as a question (turn 4), she is checking to see if anyone else has another comment to offer. This can be seen as similar to what Pimm (1987) terms *echoing*, affording the group an opportunity to add further information to the discussion.

On a few occasions, students claimed their expertise by disagreeing with the teacher or the text, as in the following example:

(1)   ANNE: (*Reading*) SOME WHALES ARE THE BIGGEST ANIMALS IN THE WORLD/
(2)   GUILLERMO: Sharks are bigger than whales.
(3)   ANNE: Guillermo, some whales are even bigger.
(4)   MONTREL: There's a book with a whale in it, Mrs. Barry. (He goes and finds a comparison chart in a book showing the relative size of whales to other animals.)

                                                                        (6/5/92)

This excerpt is a fine example of authoritative stances toward knowledge. Guillermo publicly challenges the authority of the text and shares his knowledge that sharks are even bigger than whales. Anne does not accept his contribution as accurate and uses her authority as teacher to correct Guillermo's understanding. It is interesting to note, however, that Montrel is interested in confirming this understanding of Anne's by checking with another source and quickly leaves the group to find a chart he remembered from another book. This negotiated dance of student/teacher/textual authority was often played out regarding knowledge construction in these read-alouds and became increasingly more complex as the year unfolded. That is, the instances of students claiming their expertise, both confirming and challenging the text, increased as the year progressed.

It should be noted that in all of the read-alouds transcribed over the course of the school year, there is not a single instance of a girl claiming expertise. That is, when girls initiated with information from outside the text, they did so by making links to textual authority, personal experience, or intertextual authority.

Affective Response

In contrast, girls were much more heavily represented in the final category: making an affective response. An example of this follows:

(Anne has just finished reading a section from *Koko's Kitten* [Patterson, 1991] in which Ball, the kitten, dies. There is a long, stunned moment of silence.)

(1)   MAYA: I'm ready to cry because I loved her and didn't want her to get hurt.

(2)   MONTREL: That makes you think of Soxie, right?
(3)   MAYA: That kinda looks like my cat.
(4)   ANNE: It looks like Soxie, too.

(6/15/92)

Maya initiates by sharing her personal feelings regarding the death of the kitten in the book. Montrel is quick to empathize, making the link between Ball and Maya's personal experience with her own cat, Soxie. This gives Maya the opportunity to elaborate on another connection she has made to the text (turn 3)—that the two cats look alike.

Montrel's move in turn 2 illustrates the powerful ways that children in a classroom become a community. He starts by recognizing and sympathizing with Maya's sad feelings: not making fun or "playing it off." He then legitimates her sad feelings publicly by making the link between the book cat, Ball, and her real cat, Soxie. These 6- and 7-year-olds displayed similar knowledge of one another's lives, interests, and concerns throughout the school year in various activities.

BALANCING TEACHER EXPERTISE WITH STUDENT INITIATIONS

Opening up the classroom floor to student initiations in the course of these interactive read-alouds presented particular challenges to teacher authority. In this last section, I explore particular process issues during read-alouds and how Anne dealt with when to insert her own knowledge and expertise, as well as exploring how students contested her knowledge.

As could be expected, interactive read-alouds sometimes posed management issues for Anne. When students started to speak simultaneously, Anne would often signal for quiet by raising her hand. She would then say, "This will be raising hands," to signal that the students should raise their hands and wait to be called on. The shyer, quieter children almost always raised their hands and waited to be called on before they spoke, regardless of whether she had made the announcement. Anne worked hard to protect these children's speaking rights, as can be seen in the next excerpt. Here, Yesenia raises her hand for the first time ever during a teacher-led read-aloud:

MARCOS: I know what turns into a butterfly.
CHILD 1: A caterpillar.
YESENIA: Caterpillar.
CHILD 2: Butterfly.
LOLA: Raise your hand.
ANNE: Raise your hand.

CELINA: Don't scream out.
ANNE: And don't scream out. Hang on, you've had a lot of time to talk (said to Celina). *Yesenia.*
YESENIA: I know who turns into a butterfly.
ANNE: Who does?
YESENIA: Caterpillar
ANNE: Good for you. Excellent. *Very* good.

(4/3/92)

Anne has noticed Yesenia's first effort to contribute to the discourse, and she emphasizes it exuberantly. We can see how a teacher who opens up the conversational floor to students also needs to support the access of quieter, shyer, less confident students. But this excerpt also shows that the teacher was not the only person in the room concerned about managing the students' speaking rights. Lola actually initiated the management of speaking turns by calling for hands to be raised. Celina added to this direction by reminding children not to scream out. Anne, in both cases, echoed their suggestions, thereby turning them into teacher directives. Because of this structural support, Yesenia (a child with developmental disabilities) was able to contribute her knowledge of caterpillars turning into butterflies. Her brother, Marcos, had actually initiated the topic of metamorphosis, but Anne used her authority as teacher to give Yesenia the floor. In this example, the traditional IRE pattern is turned on its head, and the student is posing her own question to be answered in public. In this way, Yesenia's first whole-class remark in the three months she had been in Room 104 can be seen as an act of procedural display: She is making her knowledge public to the classroom community.

So rather than follow the more typical routine of answering teacher-posed questions during and after a read-aloud, these students were able to initiate and direct the flow of knowledge. By allowing, and indeed encouraging, student initiations during read-alouds, Anne gained entry into some of her students' understandings. This opening up of the conversational floor to student initiations offers chances for students to question, explain, and direct. Participatory read-alouds, then, permitted students to share authority for classroom process as well as the construction of knowledge and expertise.

Yet such an opening of the floor requires that teachers decide when to intervene with their own expertise and when to listen as children struggle to develop their own. Sometimes such a sharing of authority is misconstrued by teachers to mean a withdrawal of authority. Deciding when and how to direct learning in such collaborative classrooms is an important challenge. As Wells and Chang-Wells (1992) state:

In our concern to have students take greater responsibility for their own learning, therefore, it is important that we do not mistakenly hold back from providing assistance when this is needed. On the other hand, we need to ensure that, when we offer assistance, we do so in a manner that is contingently responsive to the learners' goals and to the meanings they are constructing, and supportive of their creative attempts to make new connections and find novel solutions to problems. (p. 48)

The ways in which encouraging students to speak as experts lead to a co-construction of meaning (Wells & Chang-Wells, 1992) and a handover of knowledge and autonomy (Edwards, D., & Mercer, 1987) is the topic of the final section of this chapter. This seems to be one of the most difficult aspects of sharing authority: What is the role of the teacher regarding scaffolding students' understandings? How does Anne take her own expertise, her students' expertise, her assessment of what they need next, and then integrate all three and figure out how and what to teach next? This sharing of authority is much like recreational dancing: weaving together the partner's moves, your own moves, and the moves that are known and recognized by the world at large. Obviously most dance steps are an aspect of the sociocultural context. We learn new dance steps in part by watching and dancing with those around us. Many dances are part of particular cultures and are directly taught by one dancer to another. In this way, the teacher can be seen as knowing more dance steps of the larger sociocultural world; the teacher has specific knowledge as a more expert member of the community. And yet many of the dance steps in this classroom can also be seen as improvisational ones, in which the partners are responding to one another's spontaneous moves.

Teacher's Expert Knowledge

Turning specifically to how Anne balanced her greater expertise with the growing expertise of the children, an excerpt from the first read-aloud audiotaped is illustrative. Anne was reading *First Flight* (McPhail, 1987), a book about a boy's airplane trip to visit his grandmother. She was on the last page of the book and stopped to explain the picture showing the pilot giving the boy a miniature pair of wings:

ANNE: Pilots usually have a little pin . . it's their/
CAMILA: MY GRANDMA IS WAITING FOR ME.
ANNE: Do you know any more?
CHILDREN: MY GRANDMA IS WAITING FOR ME.
ANNE AND CHILDREN: HOW WAS YOUR FIRST FLIGHT SHE ASKED. WONDERFUL I SAY
    AND I TELL HER ALL ABOUT IT.

(11/8/91)

Anne's explanation of the meaning attached to the pilot's wings was interrupted by Camila's reading of the text. Even though the teacher was trying to provide an explanation of the text, Camila was focused on reading the book and interrupted Anne to finish reading the page. Rather than pursue her explanation about pilot wings, Anne put aside sharing her own expertise and followed the student's agenda. The teacher's prompt, "Do you know any more?" was understood by the other students as an invitation to finish reading the text, which Anne helped them to do by slowly reading the final words of the book.

As this was near the beginning of the school year, read-alouds were often an occasion for students to read out loud with the teacher and make the print connections so important for emergent readers (Sulzby & Teale, 1987). Camila, as I observed through the rest of the school year, rarely initiated during read-alouds. In fact, this was Camila's only interruption of teacher talk in over 300 pages of transcriptions. But her excitement about her emerging reading skills took precedence over her normal pattern of waiting for conversational breaks and teacher invitations to reply. Anne, on hearing Camila's excitement about being able to read the text, put aside her own agenda concerning the meaning attached to pilot's wings and followed the excitement of a group of first graders as they participated as budding experts in the magic of reading.

Essentially, Anne was sharing her authority for classroom knowledge and what would count as valid classroom procedures with her students as she followed their lead. For Anne to share her authority does not mean that she hides it and denies her expertise: She knows about the pin pilots wear and calls her students' attention to it. Yet when their attention is on the words from the book, not on the teacher's spoken words, Anne follows their lead and begins to read the last page in unison with the children. The project of reading is a shared one: a project so important to both teacher and students that she is willing to put aside her lesson on pilot's wings—gained from her own experience flying in commercial planes— to pursue the halting but excited words of a first grader impatient to learn to read.

Thus shared authority is really mutual, or mutually negotiated authority: a sense of common purpose and multidirectional respect; a promise to search for what we each know, value, and desire; an attempt to connect our texts, our interpretations, and our experiences; a willingness to check in with the "Other" and investigate what she or he is thinking. In this view of shared authority, there is not a "giving up" of authority to make room for the children's authority. Sharing authority with children does not necessitate giving up our authority as teachers. Rather, it requires us to negotiate mutual authority together.

So, too, authority was negotiated by Anne when students presented information to the group that conflicted with her own understandings. She was often able to do this by building on the words of other students, as illustrated in the following excerpt from a read-aloud of *Fiesta* (Behrns, 1978) in May:

(15)   ANNE: ON MAY FIFTH, WAY BACK IN 1862—which is about a hundred
              thirty years ago—THERE WAS A BIG BATTLE IN THE TOWN OF . . PUEBLA,
              MEXICO (with hesitation about pronunciation of "Puebla").

(16) CHILD 1: Puebla, Mexico?

(17) CHILD 2: Puebla (pronouncing it correctly)

(18) ANNE: IN A BATTLE WITH THE FRENCH ARMY, THE POOR, RAGGED MEXICAN ARMY WON A GREAT VICTORY.

(19) CHILD 2: It was a trophy that they won.

(20) ANNE: You think they won a trophy if they won a victory? When you have a/

(21) CHILD 3: They shoot 'em/

(22) ANNE: When you have a battle and you shoot and you win, that's not the same as winning a prize. Okay, a victory in a game/

(23) CHILD 3: The other one, it means they won the fight.

(24) ANNE: It means they won their fight. Let's find out about it.

(5/5/92)

In this excerpt, a child offers an explanation of "victory" that conflicted with Anne's more expert understanding of the use of victory as it applied to battles. Certainly many children struggle with multiple word meanings, but it is important to remember that over half the students in this class were bilingual—some had only learned English when they came to kindergarten or preschool.

What happened in this brief dialogue was that the teacher began to explain the distinction between a sports victory and a war victory to clarify a student's confusion (turn 20). Child 3's interruption and explanation (turn 21) was integrated into Anne's next explanation (turn 22). She used language from the text (battle and victory) and also language from child 3 (shoot). Thus, even when speaking as expert, the teacher's authority was shared by incorporating both the language of the children and the language of the text.

Contesting Teacher Knowledge

Just as a student in the transcript above corrected Anne's pronunciation of "Puebla," children did not hesitate to correct her other mistakes. Although students in Room 104 rarely contested Anne's procedural decisions, they actively disagreed with her knowledge claims—especially as the year progressed. In the following excerpt, students not only point out Anne's mistake, but check for proof that she hasn't made further errors:

(Anne has finished the read-aloud of *A Promise Is a Promise* [Munsch & Kusugak, 1988].)

ANNE: Here's a picture of Michael. He's the Inuit man who helped write the story. And here's the man who drew the pictures/

CHILD 1: That's a girl

CHILDREN: That's a girl

ANNE: <u>You can take it</u> and look at the pictures.

CHILD 2: That's a girl.

ANNE: Oh, it is a woman. (Laughing) Thank you . . uh . .

CHILD 3: Melinda.

ANNE: Someone went and got show-and-tell (Henry brings another Robert
    Munsch book over to the group from the book shelf and shows the
    author's photograph on the back cover) and it's the same Robert Munsch,
    isn't it? Henry got the book for us to show us/

MELINDA: (To Henry) Thank you. Where's the one *I Love You*? [referring to
    Love You Forever (Munsch, 1986)]

                                                                                                (2/26/92)

Anne is clearly not the sole authority in this classroom regarding interpreting
the gender of the illustrator's photograph on the back cover of this book. The
children questioned the teacher's authority by interrupting her explanation and
correcting her. They were persistent in this correction—repeating "That's a girl"
three times before Anne acknowledged them. They clearly felt confident that they
were right and she needed to be corrected, which Anne then reinforced by thank-
ing them. And Henry's retrieval of another Robert Munsch book to check his
photograph, too, can be seen as a desire to check for textual proof that this was
indeed the picture of Robert Munsch. Rather than view a child seeking verification of what the teacher said as distraction, disturbance, or defiance, Anne pointed
out to the group how Henry had contributed to their understanding. In fact, he
even received thanks from another child for his efforts.

This interchange, although delightful in its illustration of a sharing of authority for knowledge construction, was not unusual in Anne Barry's classroom. Students were encouraged by small exchanges such as this to develop their own expertise and think for themselves and with one another. Correction of teacher errors
were praised, and children were thanked when presenting textual verification. This
type of modeling by the teacher of openness to making mistakes sends a strong
message to learners: "When readers, writers, listeners, and speakers take risks,
inevitably there will be mistakes, miscues, misinterpretations, and misconceptions"
(Watson, 1989, p. 137). A teacher who actively models that authoritative stances
may be incorrect and invites children's correction creates an atmosphere of both
critical thinking and safety for risk taking so essential to active learning. This is a
shift, then, of "educational authority from without, from the experience and knowledge of the teacher, to within, to those qualities in the student" (Willinsky, 1990,
p. 192).

This requires a certain willingness to listen to children and let them direct the
work of the classroom. Anne reflected on this to the group of teachers who met
once a week: "Henry told me today, 'You have to read this book, you haven't
read it in a while.' He told me that. . . . And they catch me in my mistakes and I

laugh at my mistakes" (2/3/92). And then a year later, when reading that comment and reflecting on it, she explained:

> "They catch me at my mistakes, and I laugh at my mistakes"—I think that's important. If teachers can't do that, if they can't be humorous, you can have teachers teaching curriculum, but if you don't have those other elements, it's probably not as good. Teachers sometimes get very angry and upset when children correct them. (5/30/93)

This concept of contingent response is illustrated quite well in the dialogue during these teacher-led read-alouds presented throughout the chapter. The floor is indeed open to many student initiations, allowing students to engage in co-construction of both knowledge and process. Yet the floor is also controlled by the teacher, as she both inserts her knowledge of content and directs the process of the read-aloud. Thus teacher control allows for the legitimization of knowledge and the regulation of participation. In classrooms in which teachers strive to share authority with students, there can be no easy formula for when to step in and when to step back. It is a negotiated dance, where students sometimes lead and the teacher must learn new steps.

5

"You Could Come Read with Me"
Sharing Authority in Student-Led Read-Alouds

As has already been noted, teacher-led read-alouds were a centerpiece of the reading instruction in Anne Barry's classroom. However, the teacher was not the only member of the class who read out loud. As the year progressed, students also read out loud to the class, reading first from their journals, then group-composed texts, and finally moving on to read from children's literature trade books. This chapter examines the nature of these student-led read-alouds, the role the teacher played in this process, and ways in which authority was shared within this classroom routine.

JOURNAL READ-ALOUDS

From the very beginning of the year, at Anne's invitation, students took turns reading their journal entries to the class. Anne modeled this routine by reading her own journal entries. She wanted to show that everyone in the class can be a writer and that this writing can be shared with an audience.

The student volunteer would sit in the front of the class—in the "everything chair"—and read a selection and show the illustrations. The audience actively participated in directing these read-alouds, as illustrated in the following transcript. Also reflected here is the teacher's management of the activity to maximize the use of class time.

(1) MELINDA: Can I read my journal?

(2) ANNE: Yes, you may. Up front. This is your home journal? Some people are going to get some more at-home journals [see Chapter 7] today I promise you. So you remind me later. OK, while she's going, let's do November [Maurice Sendak's (1962) *Chicken Soup with Rice* book of poems for each month of the year]. She has to look in her backpack.

(Anne and children do choral reading of poem.)

(5) ANNE: Ready?
(6) MELINDA: MY MOM WENT TO A PARTY. I DIDN'T GET TO GO/
(7) CHILD 1: You didn't show us the pictures. (Melinda shows a picture.)
(8) CHILD 2: And the other one on back. Yeah, that one.
(9) ANNE: OK, she's going to get there.
(10) MELINDA: ME AND MY MOM WENT TO THE PARK. I LOVE MY MOM. I LOVE MY
       DAD. MY MOM IS GOING TO TAKE THE AIRPLANE TO MEXICO. MY MOM
       LOVES ME. I LOVE MY MOM.

(11/25/91)

As can be seen from this excerpt, Melinda had to solicit and obtain teacher permission to begin reading out loud to the class. This remained true throughout the entire school year, whether the child read a journal or a trade book. In addition to being in charge of scheduling, Anne can also be seen directing the use of the students' waiting time, much like a good stage manager; in this excerpt she realized (even though Melinda didn't say so) that her journal was in her backpack in the coat area. Not wanting to have "down time" for the students as they waited for Melinda, Anne directed the class in a choral reading. This points to one aspect of the teacher's major roles in a classroom: She or he can plan ahead and direct group process in a way that we would not expect a group of first graders to do for themselves. This is a good example, then, of the teacher being in authority for classroom process and not sharing it or negotiating with the students.

Moving back to the transcript, the children's comments to Melinda reflect their involvement as an audience in directing the process of the read-aloud. Both Child 1 and Child 2 were interested in seeing the illustrations that accompanied the text (turns 7 and 8). Melinda complied with their requests, acknowledging the students' authority in making such requests of readers. However, Anne offered Melinda support by negotiating with the audience (turn 9), reassuring them that she will show the pictures at the right time. This works to remind the audience that not only is the read-aloud in the hands of the reader, it is also somewhat textually controlled ("She'll get *there*"). So Anne can be seen using her authority as a teacher to intercede in Melinda's behalf.

This kind of teacher support for students negotiating with peers is a type of expertise that the teacher must delicately balance; without the adequate skills needed to assert her own authority, a child could be overwhelmed by peer comments if the teacher does not provide back-up. Hence an absence of teacher authority here would be considered as an abandonment. Yet for the teacher to intervene too much might close the door to the student learning to do her own negotiation, and it could also stifle future peer input. Thus a large part of teacher expertise in the collaborative classroom is negotiating peer input. (Later in the chapter there are excerpts that illustrate that in addition to the teacher, peers also served as experts in helping readers negotiate with their audience.)

The peer input in this transcript is purely related to the process of the read-aloud: The children requested that Melinda show the pictures to the audience. It is important to note that when students share their writings in a workshop approach, there is also room for students to comment on the *content* of the writing, not just the delivery. Timothy Lensmire (1994), in *When Children Write*, devotes an entire chapter to the riskiness children face when reading their writings out loud in a third-grade class. He reminds us that "audiences are sources of risk in the chance that they will reject the work and the author . . . [and] children in the workshop were often confronted by audiences with whom they were less than comfortable" (p. 89). Although the potential existed for children to make negative comments about another student's writing, I never heard any over the course of the school year, and Anne never mentioned this as a problem. The difference between Lensmire's third grade and Anne's first grade cannot be attributed merely to the age of the reader/writers: in her study of first-grade-age children, Anne Dyson (1989) describes one teacher's effort to make group sharing time an occasion for celebration and not allow the criticism that crept in when children worked in small groups. Such negative peer interactions were not something that Anne Barry or I observed in Room 104.

In any case, in all three classrooms, teachers can be seen actively monitoring and structuring the child-led read-aloud of personal writing. In Anne's class, members of the audience were permitted to help direct the read-aloud, at least in the process dimension. Student audience members also frequently joined the teacher in helping encourage writers to read. In this next excerpt, students were taking turns reading letters they had written to a person or character of their choice. Miriam had finished reading her letter to Goldilocks, and Anne tried to encourage Catherine to read hers:

> ANNE: Catherine, honey, would you like to read us yours? (Catherine shakes her head. Anne goes over and kneels by her desk and whispers to her. She still is shaking her head.)
> CLAUDIO: She's shy. Catherine, you want the teacher to read it for you?
> ANNE: You want a helper? (Catherine is still shaking her head.) Look how pretty it is. We want to see who you wrote to. We'll leave it here and see if you decide later to read it. She is going to decide. Claudio, come on [and read yours].

(3/18/92)

Just as Anne used her authority during teacher-led read-alouds to make room for student initiations as audience members, so, too, did she spend extra time with shyer, quieter students, encouraging them to read out loud to the class. A few children in the class seldom volunteered to read out loud, nor did they initiate with questions or comments during read-alouds. Part of the teacher's expertise, then, involves finding ways for these students to get involved in whole-group activities. In the above excerpt Claudio shared this responsibility with the teacher, by both explaining Catherine's behavior to the other children as well as trying to scaffold her participation. The teacher takes up Claudio's suggestion of having someone else read the writing and expands the offer beyond herself to include any "helper"—student or teacher. Catherine, though, is not persuaded.

In the end, however, the message from the teacher is not one of pressure, but of autonomy: "You decide." This evidences a strong commitment to author control and ownership. Anne's message of writer control was established early in the year and remained consistent throughout—see, for example, in Chapter 3, Felipe's declining to read his journal.

It is probably not coincidental that Felipe and Catherine actively declined offers to read out loud. They were students who were clearly more proficient in Spanish than in English and received supplemental ESL (English as a Second Language) instruction through a pull-out class. Their reticence to publicly share their writing, however, should not be interpreted as their not being included in the class writing community. As Anne related to the teachers' meeting later that year:

> Felipe wrote a poem about penguins . . . and now all the other children are starting to write poems using the same structure. He goes to Mrs. Clark [ESL teacher] and read it to her and shared with her how much he loves school. (2/3/92)

Finally, after weeks of editing, coaching, practicing, and student support, Felipe got up to read his penguin poem from his journal. It appears in the form in which it was published (by Anne on the classroom wall):

> Five little penguins sitting on the ice.
> The first one said, "I'm getting a fish."
> The second penguin said, "I'm going for a swim."
> The third one said, "I'm sailing on the ice."
> The fourth one said, "I'm going to jump on the ice."
> The fifth penguin said, "I'm going to get a seal."
> The penguins are the funniest creatures I've ever seen.

Felipe even chose this piece to read during the final child-led read-aloud "Celebration of Learning" held in June with parents and friends.

BOOK READ-ALOUDS

Although journals were the first writings students read out loud, in December children began reading portions of trade books out loud. This began when Anne asked for volunteer helpers to take turns reading letters in the book *The Jolly*

Christmas Postman (Ahlberg & Ahlberg, 1991). After this read-aloud, the students wrote letters to one another that got hung from a miniature tree and were read throughout the course of the month. Reading of trade books was expanded in January when Anne invited students to "practice" specific books at home and then come and read out loud to the class. This idea grew out of a concern that she expressed in the teachers' group meetings:

> Everyone takes a book home every night except on the weekend, and they have their own basal they can take if they want. And I spot check what books they're taking home so if they take the same book home all the time, I get them to try other books. But I need to spend more time reading the books with them. I need to find time to spend with them reading to me. (11/4/91)

Someone in the group mentioned a kindergarten teacher she knew who had dealt with this issue by encouraging students to read books they had practiced to the whole class. Anne remembers saying to herself, "Yeah, that's a great idea, having them practice reading the books at home and then coming and reading them to the group" (5/23/93). By February, child-led read-alouds were an established routine. Anne explained their importance:

> Look at LaToya for example, she's a kid who no one probably does much with her at home. And she's coming to me saying, "I love to read. Can I read this book to the children?" Now it's a very easy book, but she wants to read. (2/3/92)

Anne made the prerequisite for reading out loud to the whole class clear: The student needed to have practiced it ahead of time. This is reflected in Celina's read-aloud request: "Can I read *Snow* (McKie & Eastman, 1962)? I know it" (2/10/92). When Anne suspected that a student had no one with whom to practice at home, she made a point of having them practice with her, even if this meant staying after school to give quiet, undivided attention. That the teacher would be the final arbiter of who was ready to read out loud was made clear. For example, when fielding a request by a student in March, Anne replied, "Some day when I know you've practiced." So although students retained "veto power" regarding sharing their own writing with the class, the teacher was final arbiter when it came to reading published books.

Once permission had been secured from the teacher to start a child-led read-aloud, however, the reader had much control of the actual process. The reader had not only selected the book but also made minute-to-minute decisions about what would be expected from the audience. In the next four transcriptions, student control of these read-alouds is illustrated and analyzed. Integral to this student control, however, is the subtle but significant role of the teacher.

The student-led read-aloud presented below occurred at the very end of the year and was conducted by a tiny 6-year-old girl who took a very assertive role whenever she read out loud to the class. To understand what Camila starts to do in turn 8 of this excerpt, it is important to note that a typical part of many teacher-led read-alouds involved a great deal of teacher-solicited student predications about the forthcoming text. Camila tries to use this approach with the book *Where's My Baby?* (Rey, 1943), which is a book of animals and their offspring:

(Camila is sitting in the "everything chair" with the book she started reading before lunch with Catherine and LaToya as her helpers. Catherine is now in the pull-out ESL class. LaToya joins her in the chair. Anne sits in a child's chair in the back of the audience.)

(1)   CAMILA: (To Melinda) You can take Catherine's place. You don't need your chair, you can share with me.
(2)   HENRY: The same author made that book as *Curious George* (Rey, 1941).
(3)   CAMILA starts reading: WHERE'S MY BABY? (Many children talk all at once about the author and about *Curious George*.)
(4)   ANNE: I'm going to help Camila [to get the children quiet].
(5)   CAMILA: (To children) On the last page you can read with me. (Camila and LaToya put their hands up—the teacher's signal for quiet.)
(6)   ANNE: OK, keep going. (They continue reading.)
(7)   CAMILA: How many are they?
(8)   CHILDREN: Ten, four, two [shouting out all at once].
(9)   CAMILA: This is raising hands.

                                                                    (6/15/92)

Camila clearly feels in charge of this read-aloud process: She directs who her helpers will be as well as where they should sit. Camila ignores Henry's astute observation in turn 2 about the author that was sparked by the illustrations, but since the Curious George series was a favorite of the students, much discussion takes place anyway. Anne jumps in from the back of the audience, openly declaring her intention to help get the audience ready. Not to be overshadowed, Camila gives her own direction about what she expects from the audience (turn 5). Still, she feels the need to use the teacher's read-aloud signal for quiet—a raised hand. Camila is known to overuse this signal, and a little push from Anne nudges her to continue reading (turn 6).

Starting in turn 7 and continuing throughout the remainder of the 15-minute read-aloud, Camila tries to get her classmates to predict not only what animal is going to be on the next page, but how many babies will be pictured as well. The problem that she has is that there are no textual cues or patterns that would help students make any kind of reasonable predication. The only students who get the answers correct are the ones who already know the book. And Camila had said early on, "If you know, don't say."

Anne allows Camila and LaToya's questioning to continue—although Melinda is sitting with the two other girls, she does not contribute. By the end of the read-aloud, although Camila's questions are still not ones that help the students understand the book any better, with LaToya's help she has learned how to ask the question in a way that students can at least answer:

> LaToya: How many puppies do you think he gots?
> Children: (All at once) Four, five, three.
> LaToya: One at a time.
> Camila: Who thinks it is two?
> LaToya: Who thinks it is two raise your hand.
> Camila: Who thinks it's three?
> LaToya: Raise up their hand.
> Camila: Who thinks it's four, raise their hand.

The student readers have finally understood that they need to offer one choice at a time and also tell students to raise their hands. Thus Camila and LaToya have learned useful large-group questioning skills in such a context: Present one choice at a time and indicate in advance how you want your audience to respond.

The two preceding excerpts are small portions from the beginning and near of the end of a very long student-led dialogue that was frustrating to listen to as an observer. I felt impatient and wondered why Anne was allowing Camila to continue her questioning when the audience had no way of making reasonable predictions. But Anne just sat patiently at the back of the group, observing the student-led read-aloud. I was surprised afterwards to notice that Anne's willingness to cede the questioning around this book to two of her students resulted in their learning a way to talk to a group and get the group to cooperate on a task.

Even though Camila was very assertive as a reader and did not hesitate to give directions to the class, even she alludes to the teacher's authority when she needs help:

> Camila: I need one more page. That is, this one and the other one. I'll let
>   you read it. (A child gets loud and disruptive)
> Camila: Don't scream, or Mrs. Barry will get a headache.
> Anne: That's right, don't scream or I will get a headache.

(6/5/92)

As was discussed in the previous chapter, a teacher who shares her authority does not abdicate it. Even though Anne sat at the back of the group and permitted these students to read the book and question the class almost without intervention, she still remained a major player in the group, ready to be called upon as a source of authority. That is, Camila did not ask the loud student to be quiet out of obligation to her as a reader, but instead called upon the authority of the teacher. It seemed that Camila had tried everything she knew (raising her hand for quiet, involving the audience by asking them questions, cuing the class that the book was almost over and that they would get a chance to read) and when one student got particularly loud, Camila had to resort to a higher power: the teacher. So even though the floor is open to student leadership, Camila does not rely on the loud student being quiet because she has requested it: She references the needs and desires of the teacher as her claim to authority.

Camila was a very skilled and confident class leader. The next read-aloud portrays a very different kind of student-led read-aloud, with a child who doesn't have the confidence and skills of Camila. Veronica was a new arrival to the class in March and was only beginning to read from print by the end of the school year. This was the first time she had ever volunteered to read, and Anne and her peers can be seen working to reassure Veronica that she was in control of the process:

(Anne tells Veronica she can now read from *How I Wonder* [Booth, Booth, Pauli, & Phenix, 1984]. Veronica goes up to the chair. She raises her hand in the signal for quiet.)

CELINA: Look, she's raising her hand.
ANNE: Everybody's paying attention to the reader.
CHILDREN: (Many, speaking all at once) Show us the pictures.
ANNE: Give her a chance, it's her decision. A little louder, Veronica.
   (Veronica is reading the pages, which consist of one color word per
   page.)
GUILLERMO: Can we join in?
ANNE: It's up to the reader.
VERONICA: Mrs. Barry, can they? (Anne nods and the students start reading
   with her.)
VERONICA: I don't know the words. (She points to Celina, asking her to
   come up and help.)
ANNE: This time, Celina, I'm picking. Lola, you go.

(6/5/92)

In all other child-led read-alouds observed and recorded throughout the year, Anne allowed the reader to pick her or his own helper. In this case, however, she intervened and overrode Veronica's peer selection and chose a student—Lola— who wasn't able to help many students in the class but who was able to help Veronica. So here the teacher's authority can be seen as being an expert on students' individual skill levels and structuring peer support accordingly. If Anne had only been interested in fostering Veronica's autonomy as a reader, she probably would have let the reader's own selection stand. But Anne's concern was broader than that. She wanted to provide Lola an opportunity to act as a helper— a role she didn't often get when it came to child-led read-alouds.

Noncompetitive Reading

The support and encouragement the children displayed during Veronica's first public attempts to read should not go unnoticed. Celina—a very proficient reader and outspoken director of classroom activities—lends her support to this quiet, relative newcomer to the classroom community; Celina points out to the class that Veronica is trying to get their attention by raising her hand. Anne hears Celina's call to order and reinforces it. The children are remarkably respectful as an audience: They ask for pictures and ask to join in with the reading. These are normal requests made during many read-alouds. The point is that not one child attempted to denigrate Veronica for not being able to read simple color words by June of first grade. Instead, they all treated her just like they did every other person who read to the whole group.

I've puzzled over the absence of ranking and competition among the children regarding their literacy skills. Surely they were aware of one another's reading fluency (see Chapter 6 on shared reading), and public events such as read-alouds only serve to highlight the relative sophistication of different books. Yet I never heard one instance of a child claiming superiority or proclaiming another's inferiority. In the above excerpt, Veronica was able to publicly admit, "I don't know the words," and not be teased or insulted. I speculate that Anne had helped set an ethic of celebration and care about reading and one another that permeated daily classroom routines such as read-alouds. Because basal readers were not used for instructional purposes, children were not grouped by skill levels into different books. The damage of basal achievement groups became starkly obvious one February day when two children who usually attended a magnet school were put in Anne's class for the day. (This disruption was not uncommon at that time in Chicago public schools as the local, neighborhood schools served as collection points for children attending magnet schools. If the contract bus companies had problems, the local school was responsible for housing the children for the day.) The two boys walked into Room 104 while Anne and the students were out for their early morning physical education class. I was waiting their arrival and suggested the boys could get books and take a seat and wait for the class to come back; they took their thick basal anthologies out of their bookbags and moved toward chairs in the back of the room. When the class finally arrived, the two boys were greeted with enthusiasm—being neighborhood children, they were known by many. Montrel—always the talkative, inquisitive one—launched straight away into an investigation of what books the boys were reading. Montrel started with the obvious question of, "What's your book called?" The boys read the title and eagerly explained that they were almost done and would be getting a new book next week. This news did not mean much to Montrel, who did not congratulate them on this achievement. He looked fairly puzzled and tried another question to get them talking about the book: "What's it about?" Now it was the visitors' turn to look puzzled: How could you answer that question about a basal? "We're ahead of all the other groups," one of the two explained. Montrel ignored this remark and in an exasperated tone asked, "Well, then, who's the author?" The boys did not know how to answer this, so Montrel held out his hand for the book, opened to the table of contents, and began to examine the book for himself. Within a few seconds he found a selection he knew, and they started reading it out loud together. Toward the end of the same day, when children were selecting books to take home, Yesenia picked *Three Billy Goats Gruff* (Appleby, 1985). She tried to read it with me and got stuck on the first word. One of the two visitors heard her struggling, came over and said, "I've read that book. It's simple."

The two boys from the magnet school seemed to have developed different ways to talk about books than had the children in Room 104. For them, reading seemed to be a competitive event in which accomplishment is determined by finishing one reader and getting to go on to the next—and certainly both boys were proficient readers. In contrast, to the children in Room 104, reading was a community, communicative act, in which there was even room for Veronica's learning to read color words. In contrast to the comments of the visitors, that same day I asked Miriam why *Tacky the Penguin* (Lester, 1988) was such a favorite book of children in the class. She did not say it was easy to read, or that they had finished it, but rather, "It's *so* funny." This simple comment points to the ethic of care and attitude of communication that surrounded the reading process in Anne's class. This ethic helped support children to take risks, read out loud to their classmates even when, like Veronica, they didn't know all the words.

Whole-Class Texts

There were basal readers in Room 104, and at some point in the school year, children got matching copies that they put into their desks. These were even used as a whole-class text on at least one occasion when I was observing. It was an interesting process to see evolve, and it occurred during a child-led read-aloud. What follows is an edited excerpt from my field notes:

(The children file in. Two take out books and start reading to themselves.)

CHILD: Can we do journals today?
ANNE: Not right now. I'm going to come around and help you clean up and you can listen to people read.

(Ricky and Melinda raise their hands, but many others are eager to be picked and are calling out. Anne chooses Maya to read. She sits in the everything chair and reads a piece. All the children are watching her, except for LaToya, who is reading at her desk.

Anne next picks Catherine and Camila. They sit in the chair together and bring the basal reader with them. The children all take out their basals and ask what page they are going to read from. It takes a long time for Camila and Catherine to make up their minds. They first say 16 and then change to 6. Anne is busy cleaning desks but gets involved when Montrel says, "Be quiet everybody.")

ANNE: Decide, because people have to know.

(Camila and Catherine start to read [this is the first time I have seen Catherine read, and she is really reading along with Camila quite confidently]. There is plenty of confusion for the next few minutes because Camila wants to control the read-aloud and have it be hers, but because she's picked a book everyone has, all the children are reading along with her. In fact, they are reading faster than she is. When Camila stops to show the pictures, no one is interested. Montrel tells her that she doesn't need to show the pictures since they each have the book. Felipe is sharing his basal with Adrian, and Benjamin is sharing with Guillermo.)

CAMILA: We didn't say to read.

(And then again she tried on the next page: "We didn't finish reading it." [The class was ahead of them.] Anne helps Camila and Catherine negotiate the overly enthusiastic class, who are clearly getting away from their leadership. In fact, there is some pressure to read faster coming from Claudio and surprisingly from LaToya—they are both reading much faster than the others. LaToya has turned to me many times at this point and has asked if she can read to me from the basal.)

ANNE: You better get your hands up. You better look. [This is in reference to Anne's technique of raising her hand when she wants them to be quiet.]

(Camila at one point says to Anne, "Mrs. Barry you could, too." [Read, that is.] Anne goes and looks over Montrel's shoulder and joins in the group read-aloud.)

(5/29/92)

I was struck during the read-aloud by the arrangement made by both Benjamin and Felipe to share their books. Neither Adrian nor Guillermo had books, and the whole deal was negotiated so quietly and quickly that I almost missed it. This is in contrast to the dialogue that I have heard in so many classrooms when a student has forgotten her or his book and the teacher has to make elaborate arrangements to make sure the child has a book to follow along with. Here students were making those arrangements themselves out of the felt need. In fact, no one had ever even suggested that everyone might want to follow along in their readers. It actually did not fit into Camila's plans; rather, it arose as a spontaneous group activity when the readers came to the front of the class with the basals. By the end, Camila had stopped fighting the audience and had even invited Anne to join in.

I was impressed with the students' enthusiasm for this read-aloud project they had invented for themselves. Anne had never used the matched basals as group reading books, but the students all had copies and sometimes used them during shared reading or took them home. They had done choral reading of poems and of pieces of group-composed writing, so the task of reading all at once together was not novel. What was so fascinating to watch from the back of the room was how a group activity just emerged from the child-led read-aloud. No one suggested it, and Camila even tried to discourage it, but the group had an unarticulated agenda of its own that the teacher was invited to join. This process presents quite a contrast to the image of the exhausted city school teacher wearily attempting to get her class to read out loud from a lifeless basal reader!

DIFFERENTIAL TREATMENT

In analyzing why students like Veronica were not teased by other children and were able to take public risks and ask for help, it is important to note that Anne did not try to pretend that she expected the same behaviors from every student in the class. In fact, Anne demonstrated repeatedly throughout the year that students were not treated the same. This differential reinforcement had a strong influence on the class—an influence that wasn't always very obvious at first glance. Students picked up on Anne's comments and made decisions that evidenced the power she had on shaping children's selection of peers. The following transcription, on which the opening vignette of the book was based, demonstrates this as well as showing the way in which students were differentially reinforced by the teacher. It is clear in what follows that Anne had different expectations for different students' roles as audience members in a child-led read-aloud:

(1) ANNE: I promised Marcos something. (Marcos comes up to the special chair.)

(2)   CELINA: But he doesn't know that one.

(3)   ANNE: Excuse me, he read it to me yesterday after school. He's quite
        ready, and I promised him.

(4)   (Marcos reads *Hop on Pop* [Seuss, 1963], including the cover and the
        title page. He is confident, smiling, making eye contact with his
        audience, and showing each picture to everyone in the room.
        Marcos pauses, stuck on the words.)

(5)   MONTREL: WE PLAY.

(6)   (Anne gives him "The Look" and mouths, "It's his turn." Marcos
        continues reading and pauses a little later, again not knowing the
        words.)

(7)   RICKY: GOODBYE THING. YOU SING TOO LONG.

(8)   ANNE: Great, Ricky. (Marcos continues to read a few more pages.)

(9)   MARCOS: Ricky, you could come over here and read with me. (Ricky
        bolts out of his chair and is up to the front in a flash. Marcos and
        Ricky continue reading the book.)

(10)   MARCOS AND RICKY: THAT ONE IS MY OTHER BROTHER.

(11)   MONTREL: "Other, brother" rhymes. (Anne smiles and nods.)

                                                                    (2/27/92)

As I watched this event unfold in the classroom, I was immediately intrigued by Marcos's ownership of the read-aloud. As mentioned in the introduction of this book, Marcos and Ricky handled their own negotiation of the read-aloud: Marcos asked Ricky for help and he complied. Ricky was not a student who usually participated in group activities. In fact, during most child-led read-alouds, Ricky had a different book hidden halfway inside his desk that he read while the class was hearing something else. On most days, it seemed as if Ricky made sure he was always doing something different from what was expected of him by the teacher. If he was supposed to be in small groups, Ricky worked alone. If it was silent reading time, Ricky went to talk about his book to another student. If it was teacher-led read-aloud time, Ricky did his math worksheet. If it was journal time, Ricky was doing silent reading.

So Anne's comment to Ricky in turn 8 ("Great, Ricky") must be understood in light of Ricky's usual resistance to the expected activity. Ricky was following along with a group activity for a change. But just a second earlier in turn 6, Montrel was negatively sanctioned with "The Look" and a silent admonition of "It's his turn." Both boys were exhibiting the exact same behavior: helping the reader out by offering the words. Yet Montrel was told to be quiet and Ricky, while doing the *exact same thing* a few turns later, was praised. Anne's negative response to Montrel did not seem to discourage him from making a further contribution in turn 11, and this time he received a positive smile and a nod.

Anne's responses to the students' comments can be read as contributing to Marcos's request for Ricky to join him as his helper. I asked Marcos right after this read-aloud why he invited Ricky to join him. He said, "He was helping me."

"Do you mean he was helping you learn the book yesterday?" I asked.

"No," Marcos explained, "he was helping me from his desk."

As *Hop on Pop* was a big favorite of many of the students in Room 104, other children besides Montrel and Ricky were also saying some of the words as Marcos read them. However, as Ricky was the only child that Anne publicly praised for this assistance, it seems probable that it was this teacher approval that drew Marcos's attention to Ricky's "help from his desk." So even in a process which at first glance appears to be very child-controlled, the teacher's voice is one that carries much weight and influence.

This influence can be seen earlier in the transcript, too: In turn 3 Anne addresses Celina's concern that Marcos is not ready to read the book. She uses her authority as teacher ("I promised him") but also takes Celina's concern seriously by offering her an explanation of how she knows he is ready. Anne does not say, "I decide who gets to read," but rather responds to the substance of Celina's concern and reassures her that Marcos has indeed met the prerequisite of practicing ahead of time. Although authoritative and unwavering, the teacher's comment can be read as legitimating Celina's concern in that Anne directly addressed the substance of the child's issue.

CHILDREN'S LEADERSHIP

Throughout this chapter, children's comments during child-led read-alouds have pointed to the children's comfort with giving one another process directions but not passing judgment. Children did not negatively comment on other students' writing, nor did they remark on peer competencies in oral decoding of text. The student audience interjected frequently during child-led read-alouds about who should get to read, how the person should read, and who should read with them. Students even encouraged and supported shy and reluctant readers, offering suggestions such as selecting a helper or helping get the audience quieted down. Furthermore, the actual reader regularly took charge of the process: calling on classmates as helpers, telling the audience when they could read along, and asking the audience to make predictions. Yet through all of this student-directed process, the teacher, although most often at the back of the room, remained available as an authoritative resource.

To fully appreciate the power of the children's actions of direction and leadership during read-alouds in Room 104, it is important to point out that among the children seen directing the work in this classroom, one was labeled emotionally disturbed; one was developmentally disabled; one had turned 8 in the spring of first grade; one came into first grade unable to put together a six-piece jigsaw puzzle and not knowing how to cut with scissors; one was living in a home with a drug-addicted mother who gave birth to a baby that spring alone in the bathtub with the first grader as her only helper; one missed almost half the year of school days—in part, when her mother took her to Mexico; one was living with an elderly grandmother; one student's father was in prison; and five new students had arrived in the spring.

These are not the typical students usually offered pedagogies that foster group communication and leadership. Too many urban teachers feel a need to tightly control instruction and not leave any room for students to lead and for teachers to sometimes follow. I often tell a vignette from another Chicago public school that illustrates a common ideology. I was supervising student teachers and needed to talk to the European American host teacher of a third-grade class of all African American children. I had not been able to reach the teacher either before school or after school and arrived just as class was beginning. The teacher agreed to talk to me after she got the class going, so I sat in the back of the room for a few minutes. She told the class, "You have your work, and Ms. Marsh [not her real name] is in charge. *Whatever Ms. Marsh tells you to do, you do!*"

Afterwards I asked Ms. Marsh whether, if she had told them to jump out of the window, they would have been expected to jump. My point is the need to work against the destructive presence of poisonous pedagogy present in some urban classrooms. Teachers bent on controlling students' behaviors actively require them not to think and evaluate or question or initiate. Rather, a premium is placed on following directions and complying with outside authority. This form of pedagogy, although it might attempt to train obedient and compliant citizens and workers, is inherently antidemocratic. In contrast, the students in Room 104 were exploring ways to negotiate their own authority, not with the absence of the teacher and her authority, but with its productive presence. I am reminded of Paulo Freire's (1994) advice:

> To teach democracy, we must have this taste for democracy, which entails many other tastes, such as a taste for risk-taking, a taste for adventures, a taste for being and experiencing oneself constantly in uncertainties. . . . This taste for democracy is not innate. . . . But, since we are agents of change within our culture, we must also be the creators of this taste for democracy. And sometimes we must create this taste against the very power of our culture. (p. 117)

If our culture is insisting—as it sometimes is—that poor children of color should be educated to comply rather than question, and follow rather than lead, we must actively disrupt this notion wherever we find it. As the students and teacher in Room 104 so ably demonstrate, classrooms can be sites for the practice of individual and collective decision making, initiative, and leadership.

6

"Me and Marcos Know"

Negotiating Knowledge and Process in Buddy Reading

One day in Room 104 Anne stepped out of the classroom to attend to some business in the office. She didn't announce her exit, and not one child seemed to notice. The students were so intently engaged reading their books, poems, charts, and posters that the teacher's absence did not disrupt this work. Children were found throughout the room: Lola and Maya were at the chalkboard choral reading poems as Montrel used the long pointer to mark the words; others were clustered in pairs and trios with matched books reading out loud together; Melinda and Celina were sitting at their individual desks with their heads buried in books; Silvia, Valentina, and George were grouped around the kidney-shaped table standing as they read a Big Book together; Felipe and Adrian were searching through one of the many bookshelves for a book on dinosaurs they wanted.

This chapter investigates how students shared authority during the process of shared, or buddy, reading. It was during this routine that the students were most free to negotiate with one another for both classroom space and text selection. As expressed by the chapter title—"Me and Marcos know"—students used shared reading to develop expertise alone and with one another. The very nature of the activity meant that the teacher could not possibly monitor what every child was doing, thereby creating room for student authority.

SHARED AND BUDDY READING

The term "shared reading" has been used in many whole-language classrooms to describe the process of the teacher's sharing Big Books with students (Holdaway, 1979). Anne, however, used the term "shared reading" to mean free reading that occurred almost daily and involved student selection of text, location to read, and partner(s). Students sometimes read alone but often picked "buddies":

> Buddy reading acknowledges the social nature of reading by having children pair up. . . . Children take turns reading different books, or pages of the same book. Buddies do not have to be at the same reading level, because they are selecting their own material. (Pappas et al., 1995, p. 246)

Although the format for shared (or buddy) reading stayed consistent through-out the year, one change emerged in December that grew directly out of student initiation. As mentioned in Chapter 3, the scheduling of shared reading changed over the year. From the very first day of school, as students finished writing in their journals and drawing pictures, they would go to the back of the room and select books and buddy read. However, by the second half of the year, shared reading also happened first thing in the morning as students and teacher got orga-nized for the day. This change, which Anne later incorporated as part of her ex-pectations, emerged from the students' own initiation. Anne explains:

> I've been noticing that the morning time now when homework is being collected and pencils are sharpened that the children are now reading their books that they've taken home. They're doing lots of rereadings. It's just kind of happened, and I feel good about it because it's a good use of what used to be sort of wasted time. They come in, get organized, and sit down and read. (12/16/91)

So here is an example of children sharing authority for classroom process: who gets to do what, where, when, and how. This sharing occurred quite spon-taneously and did not require teacher negotiation to get it started. It is concrete example of the teacher "leading from behind," that is, following the lead of the children. The students' initiation (to use the early morning business time to read) made sense to Anne, so she used her authority as teacher to formalize the use of this early morning time as an occasion to read. Only a month later it can be seen that this informal initiation of some students had become a suggested activity:

(Ricky, a new student, is sitting at his desk and still has his coat on and bookbag on his desk.)

(1)   ANNE: While you're waiting you may either read your book or/
(2)   CHILD 1: Mrs. Barry, can I hang up my coat?
(3)   CHILD 2: Teacher, can I go sharpen?
(4)   ANNE: Camila and those three people, hurry up. If you're waiting, you could be looking at your books. Ricky, come here, I want to show you something. You're row three and you need to be over here. (Ricky goes into coatroom as Anne directs him.)
(5)   CELINA: Teacher, look where I'm at [in the basal reader].
(6)   ANNE: You're that far? Good for you.
(7)   CELINA: Can I buddy read with Claudio for a little while?
(8)   ANNE: Can you buddy read with Claudio?/

(9)   CELINA: <u>For a little while because</u> he knows. His mom was helping
          him with some of the words.
(10)   MONTREL: (To Henry) Can you buddy read with me?

                                                                    (1/30/92)

Anne's use of "you may read your book" (turn 1) and "you could be looking at
your books" (turn 4) are directions regarding class process and are couched as
invitations to read. She begins in turn 1 to offer a choice of activities but is interrupted by students requesting permission to sharpen pencils and hang up coats.
The general rule of the classroom (which I didn't figure out until Ricky arrived in
January and didn't follow it) was that students should not get out of their seats
without permission. This was not true, however, in shared reading, during which
students moved freely around the room.

Returning to Anne's use of invitational language rather than direct orders, it
should be noted that these suggestions to read could be seen as commands
that have been couched in the language of politeness (Cazden, 1988; Manke,
1993; White, 1989). What points away from this analysis and suggests that
Anne's invitations here were genuine and could be declined is how Anne gives
explicit commands later in the year during another early morning getting-settled
time:

(All children, except for Claudio, are reading. They are in pairs, groups, or
alone.)

ANNE: Claudio, I want you to get a book. (Claudio reaches for a book from
    Ricky's desk.)
CLAUDIO: Mrs. Barry, look at all the books that Ricky took.
ANNE: (To Ricky) Hon, take about two of them. Claudio, *get a book.*

                                                                    (5/5/92)

As can be seen from this transcript, by May the routine of early morning shared
reading was firmly established as an expectation, not an option, as it had been
earlier in the year when it was just evolving to its additional place in the day's
schedule. (Remember that shared reading also took place as students finished
writing their individual journals.) It can be seen, then, that students helped create
this new time for shared reading in addition to the time that the teacher had sched-
uled. Students, therefore, can be seen as directly sharing authority for classroom
process. The teacher, however, used her authority to formalize this ad hoc process and make it an expectation for all students in the classroom. In this way Anne
has become one of the many teachers who

find their role changing from that of an instructor who constantly assumes responsibility for children's learning by controlling it and correcting it, to that of a facilitator who provides children with the opportunity to take responsibility for their own learning in stimulating and enjoyable ways. (Doake, 1985, p. 96)

By following the students' lead, Anne helped to foster a group feeling and sense of collective action. This is similar to the group action also evident during child-led read-alouds when the entire class took out their matching basal readers. During that time, too, Anne followed up on the student's invitation—to read with them, in that case. For classroom teachers it is important to notice when students initiate in ways that can work for smooth and enjoyable functioning of the group. As teachers we are presented with multiple opportunities such as these to share authority with students in directing the work of the classroom.

PEER INTERACTIONS IN SHARED READING

The very structure of shared reading required that students take responsibility for their own learning. Anne usually sat in one location (unless she was conferencing with individual students on their writing), and some children often elected to sit near her and ask for help as they needed it. Generally, however, students negotiated with one another to buddy read, often making as many as three or four different peer arrangements during a half hour or so of shared reading time. Most times these negotiations were in the form of invitations, like this one from Montrel to Marcos: "Could you read that book? Want me to read it?" (6/16/92).

Many negotiations for buddy reading were also done in the context of a specific book, with students demonstrating remarkable knowledge of one another's interests as well as where certain books were located on the numerous shelves. Students actively assisted each other, as reflected in Henry's offer to Camila: "Want me to find the Care Bear book for you?" Camila nodded, and they searched the shelves until they found it. This type of cooperation and concern for one another's interests was not a rare event, but was the norm.

Students often used the shared reading time to develop content expertise with their peers. In the following excerpt, three boys are looking at a very sophisticated book about the planets:

FELIPE: What are these names?
CLAUDIO: I know some of them. That's Mars.
HENRY: And Pluto/
CLAUDIO: That one's the smallest.
FELIPE: What's that one?
CLAUDIO: Umm . . Jupiter . . and . . . Mercury and/

HENRY: Venus! And Saturn. Look at all the rings/
CLAUDIO: I saw a show on TV about the planets. Mrs. Oyler, how do you
say this one? . . . Er-ay-nus?

(6/16/92)

As I listened in, the three boys went on for the next 10 minutes pooling their
rather extensive knowledge about the planets in our solar system. They shared
information they knew from television as well as calling attention to certain pas-
sages in the text. As this was a very difficult book—with small print and many
multisyllabic words—I was surprised at their persistence and comprehension. It
was clear that peer assistance, encouragement, and interest scaffolded the students'
abilities to interact with the text and gain meaning from the words. This brief interchange provides important evidence that children can indeed learn from and with
each other, even if the teacher is not directing the content or the process. Furthermore, the entire exchange was initiated by a student, demonstrating students'
abilities to identify their own needs and seek assistance.

Anne was often unaware of all the students were learning during shared reading until they introduced their content knowledge into other activities. The following excerpt from a teacher-led read-aloud illustrates how important this
expertise acquired during shared reading was to students:

MONTREL: Me and Marcos know a book about dinosaurs.
ANNE: Did you find it in my bookcase?
MONTREL: Yeah, Marcos did.
MARCOS: That's tyrannosaurus rex.
ANNE: You wanna come up and show us? I think that would be nice. Do
you wanna show us which one is tyrannosaurus rex?
MONTREL: Me and Marcos know.
MARCOS: This is tyrannosaurus rex. He eats meat. That's triceratops. That's
a/
MONTREL: Pterodactyl.
MARCOS: Yeah, pterodactyl.

(4/3/92)

This exchange illustrates how students used shared reading to interact with each
other purposefully about content of their choice. That Montrel states twice, "Me
and Marcos know," indicates how much he values this knowledge that they have
acquired together. Anne validates this common knowledge and invites the students to share their information with the class. Such teacher response to student
knowledge gained outside of large-group activities serves to invite other children
at later points to bring their own connections back to the entire class. Thus, not
only is the student initiation of making the intertextual connection valued, but the

group is enriched by the contributions of its members. A body of "common knowledge" (Edwards, D., & Mercer, 1987) is constructed.

In a way, making room for students to share their knowledge with the class actually extends Anne's authority by providing her more information about her students' interests and abilities. By allowing students to enter their comments into the discourse of the classroom, Anne has more control—not less—of the curriculum and students' understandings. Sharing authority with students can work to deepen the teacher's knowledge of students and thereby extend her authority and expertise, rather than restrict it.

This is an excellent example from daily classroom life illustrating how power and authority are not possessions in a zero-sum game. That is, by allowing students time to learn with peers through buddy reading, Anne does not lose authority because she does not know what is going on. In fact, by opening the classroom floor to invite students' knowledges into the community discourse, Anne actually gains more knowledge about her students as learners. By sharing authority, she has gained authority.

TEACHER NEGOTIATION OF PEER INTERACTION

The students who chose to buddy read, rather than read alone, usually worked out arrangements among themselves. It was not unusual, for instance, to see two girls sharing the special "everything chair" but reading two different books. Such agreements were normally made fairly quietly and quickly. However, sharing chairs and sharing turns was almost never as much of an issue as was sharing books. On these occasions the teacher was sought out to act as arbiter, as in the following examples:

> VERONICA: (To Marcos) Give me *Over in the Meadow* (Carter, 1992). We had it first. I'm gonna tell the teacher. Mrs. Barry, he had *Over in the Meadow*.
> MARCOS: I was reading it.
> ANNE: When you finish, will you give it to her?
>
> (6/16/92)

> LATOYA: Ricky has a book, and he won't give it to me.
> ANNE: Can you share?
>
> (5/5/92)

These brief excerpts indicate some of the ongoing problems students had in the shared part of shared reading. This, then, was a skill that required teacher expertise and authority. The problem of sharing books became more serious at the end of the day on Mondays through Thursdays when children were invited to go to the back of the room and select two books to take home. (Most books did not circulate on Friday afternoons because Anne was concerned that the books—which she had mostly purchased from her own money—would be harder to remember to bring back after a weekend. She had a special box of books she didn't mind losing that could go home on Friday nights. Anne did not have a written system to keep track of the books that went home, but reported that she did not think she lost even one book the entire year.) Often, because it was one of that day's read-alouds, a certain book would be quite popular, and students would try to be the first to get it. Here, Anne would intervene and work out a verbal schedule so that students could take turns. Anne's authority for book distribution extended also to her scrutiny of what students chose, as can be seen in her direction to the class: "Take a book you can read, and take one that you have to work on. Then I'm going to look" (2/10/92). Yet Anne did not just observe book choice; she actively intervened on many occasions.

Indeed, Anne consciously promoted an interest in certain books by her selection for teacher-led read-alouds. She felt that one of her purposes in that activity was to introduce plenty of predictable books (Rhodes, 1979) that the students could then practice:

> I read to them all throughout the day and hope that they will want to take the book home and read it. At least one of the books I read each day is easy enough to read. They bug each other to read the books, and the better readers will help the others. (5/18/92)

Thus Anne counted on sparking student initiation to assume responsibility for their own learning as well as share the pleasure and excitement of reading with their classmates. Thus shared reading is a routine whose very success depended on a sharing of authority—for it to work well, students had to interact, make decisions, and work together. Furthermore, it was upon such peer involvement that Anne built her reading program. The importance of peer interactions was readily apparent, for example, in a particular student's success in learning to read. LaToya was a child with many problems in her home life that left her without many of the skills the other children had. The first month of school I watched her struggling over how to put a six-piece jigsaw puzzle together. Her journal writing consisted of stringing together mostly random letters until at least February. However, by the end of the school year during the "Celebration of Learning," although no one from her family came to hear her, LaToya volunteered to go first and confidently and fluently read a fairly complex book, *Morris the Moose* (Wiseman, 1959). In speaking about LaToya's success, Anne discussed the importance of peers reading together and her own role as teacher:

> She has all those other children around her who read to her or with her or around her. So she knows she can go and pick a book up with nudging from

me—a type of book that she can read, or get someone else to read with her. She is *motivated* by the books, by the invitations in the room, by all the other children around her. Not by me so much. I'm nudging from behind. The key is the role modeling. (2/3/92)

So the teacher's job here, to teach students how to read—which is so important in first grade—is shared with students. Anne recognizes the value of peer interaction that is well documented in educational research. For instance, in one large-scale study of fifth-grade classrooms in the Chicago area, researchers found children's involvement to be highest when they were working cooperatively (Stodolsky, 1988). In classrooms where teachers foster peer interaction, there are more student-initiated questions and evaluations, along with a dominance of substantive talk about texts (Tierney & Rogers, 1989). Finally, peer feedback provides numerous opportunities for students to restructure and modify their cognitive schemas (Pappas et al., 1995).

Despite the positive aspects of peer collaboration, such a plethora of peer interaction during shared reading nonetheless created certain problems for Anne. She talked about two of these issues one November day during her 20-minute lunch break:

I'm trying to get used to the noise level and monitor them. So this is where the fine line is. The power, where I have to say to them, I want you with a book for three to five minutes. I don't want them just picking up a book and then kind of being haphazard about it or not reading or not nudging them forward and upward. (11/25/91)

As the year progressed, the noise level (which you will remember from Chapter 2 was one of Anne's greatest fears) did not in fact often become an issue. Children frequently monitored themselves fairly well, as illustrated in the following excerpt:

(Montrel and Silvia are in the front of the room reading the Big Book version of *Mrs. Wishy-Washy* [Cowley, 1980] propped up on the ledge. Silvia is using the pointer. Lola joins in using a very loud voice.)

MONTREL: (To Lola) Shh, not so loud, you have to use a quiet voice.
(5/20/92)

Anne's other concern regarding monitoring students' reading was not as easily settled as was the issue of noise level. Throughout the year, Anne had to give specific directions regarding her expectations for sticking with a book: "Three to five minutes with a book. I don't want to see you playing. I'm going to time you back there, so everyone has a turn." This problem of monitoring was a broader one than just getting children to stick with a book.

Anne struggled to find ways to better identify and assess individual students' progress. This was not an area that she resolved during the year I spent in her class. In her words, "I'm not able to monitor the kids reading as much as I would like to. I noticed that when Celina read to you she wasn't as familiar with the book as I would have expected. I've got to figure this part out better" (3/6/92). This points to one of the tensions of loosening teacher control of student learning. A sharing of power is rooted in the belief that by being less dependent on the teacher as the source of authority, students will become more autonomous (Pimm, 1987). And this indeed occurred. The classroom was transformed in important ways by students having more freedom. The changes were multiple and could be seen in small ways, such as students having time to read bulletin boards. Anne explains:

> I have always used that kind of a bulletin board [talking about the holiday poems displayed] but they never used it. They didn't have time and they weren't walking around. Now they have the freedom to look. Celina was standing over there today reading them all. (12/16/91)

Yet this very freedom creates the need for the teacher to find new ways to assess and track student progress. In classrooms where peer interactions are fostered and students are encouraged to develop direction and purpose for their own and one another's learning, there are inherent questions for teachers who must assess this learning. Not only do teachers need specific information about individual students' growth for them to be able to scaffold future learning, but they are also accountable to parents and the principal for carefully documenting student progress. This makes the risk of changing one's practice all that much harder. As Anne often said, "I hope I'm doing the right thing." In my work with preservice and practicing teachers on alternative curriculum development, I have noticed it is usually the most experienced teachers who worry first about assessment and accountability. If all the old measures are no longer being used—such as chapter tests, workbook page accuracy, and spelling quizzes—then new systems of documentation and evaluation are needed.

PUTTING DOWN THE BOOKS

For beginning teachers, one aspect of teaching they first struggle with is the transition between activities. As discussed earlier in this chapter and in Chapters 3 and 5, students often took the initiative to start reading and writing activities.

However, they did not usually take such an initiative in ending them. That burden fell almost exclusively on Anne's shoulders, and in this area she sometimes met with student resistance. What follows was not atypical when the announcement to end shared reading came:

> ANNE: Book time is over.
> CAMILA: I was reading *Chicka Chicka Boom Boom* [Martin & Archambault, 1989].
> ANNE: Isn't reading fun? (Camila returns to her seat looking rather glum.)
> (3/18/92)

Here Anne can be seen acknowledging Camila's pleasure about the book but ignoring her indirect request to continue reading. In this negotiation over ending shared reading, Anne very consistently employed the politeness strategies mentioned earlier in this chapter. As Manke (1993) explains:

> Politeness formulas . . . [include]: questions-in-place-of-commands; statements of preference in place of commands; and requests which use please, thank you, excuse me and similar words and/or are expressed conditionally (using the modals would or could) when commands could have been used. (p. 10)

Listen as Anne tries to get Melinda to end buddy reading and join the group activity: "Melinda, I know you love to read, but could you come over here now?" (3/6/92). This is an example of Anne's frequently used modal *woulds* and *coulds* in her requests to students to end shared reading. There were many times, especially in the second half of the year, when Anne either ignored or didn't notice students continuing to read at their desks when the class had gone on to a group activity. Other times, she would give the student "The Look" or gesture to put the book away. Even this was not always successful, and a student would continue to read, sometimes by placing the book inside her or his desk. Thus students who continued to read past the time for shared reading can be seen as actively contesting the teacher's authority for classroom process.

Flagrant contestation of the teacher's authority and/or classroom rules usually had a specific consequence in Anne Barry's classroom: warnings with the perpetrator's name written on the blackboard, and then after three such warnings, a time-out in the "drop-down" chair. Although I witnessed various occasions in which students were directed to this chair in the back of the room, I never saw even a warning given for reading a book when the class was doing another activity. Although at times Anne treated reading a book when the class was doing something else as a serious offense (as can be seen in the next excerpt), it still never earned a negative consequence:

(Camila is reading in front of the class.)

ANNE: (To Celina) That's what I call cheating—reading your own book while someone is reading to the class. We have plenty of time later, tomorrow, next week/
MONTREL: Next month.

(2/27/92)

Anne's definition here of "cheating" was repeated on a few occasions throughout the year's observations, always in the context of a student either reading or writing at her or his individual desk while another student was reading to the entire class. In this way, Anne used her authority to highlight the importance of respecting the student reader. Anne never, however, referred to students as cheating if they were doing the same set of behaviors while *she* read to the class. In fact, when a child—usually Ricky—did not come to the circle for the teacher-led read-aloud, he would be invited a few times, but never pressured or punished for not coming. This points to the weight Anne attached to the role of peer support and interaction in students' emergent literacy.

Although Anne had to initiate ending shared reading, students regularly did assume major responsibility for one aspect of its ending. Every time I walked into the classroom, the hundreds and hundreds of books were almost always neatly arranged on shelves, desks, racks, and tables. Students seemed to understand the categorization system (although I never did) and helped maintain it. Anne cued and directed this process constantly:

ANNE: Listen carefully. If you have a dinosaur book, put it back on the left side of Adrian's desk.
MONTREL: (Holding a dinosaur book) How many chapters does this book have? I want to see.
ANNE: Not now, Montrel. No. I'll give you time later. If you have a book that comes from the bookcase, put *just* that book, exactly where you found it.

(6/15/92)

Surprisingly, students seemed to take putting books back in the correct place very seriously. They often reminded one another, as in this excerpt during one shared reading time:

(Felipe is holding and examining a big poster of skeletons he found on a bookshelf.)

HENRY: You gotta put it back where you found it.
CLAUDIO: You're not supposed to do that. Put it away.

(6/16/92)

This system of book organization was not one the students had helped design; it was designed by Anne and utilized by the students without observable contestation. In fact, students cooperated with her plan by keeping each other in line, as Henry and Claudio did in the above excerpt.

In conclusion, then, the smooth efficiency of shared reading was due in large part to students' acceptance of Anne's system and authority. First and foremost, however, the students were motivated by an agenda they held in common with the teacher; that is, the excitement and pleasure they experienced for the very process of becoming literate. This is captured best by Valentina's comment one day to me as she showed me a copy of *Little Red Hen* (McQueen, 1985): "I took this book home and my sister came up to me and said, 'You can read?'. And I said, 'Of course.'"

Valentina's sense of pride and competence regarding her ability to read was fostered by the sharing of authority that occurred during buddy reading. In this classroom routine, students were able to develop their expertise with peers that they were then frequently able to share with the large group. Part of the authority that students shared in this activity was regarding their peers' interests and expertise. They regularly initiated shared reading with specific goals in mind: sometimes choosing a peer because of her or his expertise with a particular book; often searching for a particular book to continue reading on a topic of interest. Students also shared authority for the process of buddy reading, both by negotiating with one another for partners and positions and by adding an extra period of shared reading to the early morning routine. Such a sharing of authority within this activity presented specific concerns for Anne as teacher. She continued to explore ways to better monitor and assess student progress during shared reading. Some of these issues regarding when and how to assess students' growth can be seen also in the routine of journal writing, which is addressed in the next chapter.

7

"That's Not What I Meant"
Authorship and Authority in Individual Writing

In a democracy, education should prepare each of us to tell our own stories.
                    —Jo Anne Pagano, Exiles and Communities

On the very first day of school Anne gave each student a brightly colored spiral notebook to use as a journal. Journals quickly became a favorite activity for students, who sometimes got the class started writing without even negotiating with the teacher. This chapter examines the use of journals throughout the year, tracing how the process became increasingly social and also expanded beyond the autobiographical writing so typical of the journal format. The main focus, however, is on a nagging question Anne kept returning to throughout the year; that is, what should be her role regarding control and direction in the writing process? How much should come from the children, and how much should she propose in advance? This question can be seen as integral to an exploration of shared authority in the classroom; even in the very word *authority* lies the root *author*. Therefore, what is the role of teacher authority in helping students to author their own texts?

TEACHER AUTHORITY AND SPELLING

That students should be the authors of their own texts is central to the writing-process approach that Anne embraced (Atwell, 1987; Calkins, 1983, 1986; Graves, 1983; Smith, 1982). The theory underlying journal writing is that children learn to write by composing texts (with both words and pictures) that are meaningful expressions of their experiences, thoughts, and ideas. In a process approach, the emphasis is first on meaning and communication rather than on mechanics and form. One ramification this had was that Anne did not supply correct spellings when students requested but instead encouraged them to use invented spellings (Temple, Nathan, Burris, & Temple, 1988) and concentrate on getting their ideas

99

down on paper. Therefore, Anne used her authority as teacher to impose a process approach to classroom writing and to withhold information that students requested. She was using her expert knowledge of emergent writing to focus students on the message aspects of writing, that is, writing is used to communicate. This stance of Anne's, then, can be seen as an authoritative one—one that was not open to negotiation or sharing.

It was, however, sometimes contested. Most of the students in Room 104 had little trouble accepting the idea that they could write in their journals using invented spelling. For example, Henry's first journal entry at the beginning of September was "iLGbb" (see Figure 7.1). Conferencing later with the teacher, Henry told Anne it said, "I like green bananas," which she wrote under his entry. (*Green Bananas* is a book by Neville and Butler [1984].) The students readily accepted that they could write and were eager and able to tell Anne what their writing said. Anne printed conventional spellings underneath the children's invented ones. As individual children's encoding skills progressed, she printed fewer words under theirs.

However, in January, when five new students came into the room, some of them were puzzled by this form of writing. Ricky in particular resisted the teacher's directive that students could write without having the spelling be correct. He agonized over every word and constantly asked for help on spelling. One day in February, he came to show me his journal, which had elaborate drawings of penguins. Printed underneath were neatly written, perfectly spelled sentences. Ricky showed me the page with obvious pride and confided, "I don't like to write any ideas that aren't spelled right." I asked him, "Does Mrs. Barry say you have to spell right?" "No," he replied, "She says spell it any way you can."

Even though Ricky understood the teacher's expectations in regard to spelling, he refused to cooperate and insisted on spelling all of his ideas "right." Although Ricky was not willing to accept invented spelling, he had, however, come to believe the underlying point: that writing is about communicating one's *ideas*. Further, he had become aware of the convention, realizing the social nature of the process: People have to be able to read your writing if it is to communicate.

AUTHOR CONTROL

Such a willingness to commit one's ideas to paper is fostered by author control. Anne set up from the beginning student ownership of their own writing (see Chapter 6 on students reading journals aloud to the class): "I tell them it's *your* writing. I've been writing in my journal and read to them what I write" (9/23/91). The links among authorship, control, and public participation have implications beyond just learning to write. As Willinsky (1990) has noted:

September 12 1991

iLGbb

I like green bananas.

FIGURE 7.1. Henry's First Journal Entry

> The New Literacy encourages a more active voice for students that they might become outspoken on the page and in class. This further enfranchises students, giving them the power to actively write (and read) their own story, to feel a part and to participate in this public community of discourse and texts. (p. 30)

So by introducing journals into her classroom for the first time in 20 years of teaching, Anne did more than just foster a love of writing; she opened the door for students to "tell their own stories" (Pagano, 1990, p. 2) and created an audience to hear them. In this way, by making journals a required part of her students' curriculum, Anne used her authority as teacher to *extend* the authoring, and thereby authority, of her students.

As described in Chapter 3, students were quite fond of "doing journals" and often clamored to write. The following excerpt illustrates this process negotiation and also shows how common knowledge in this routine was built among the children:

> (Children are back from the group trip to the bathroom and are seated at individual desks set up in rows.)

> CHILDREN (lots of them): Can we do journals?
> ANNE: How about if we do our journals first?
> CHILDREN: Yeah!
> ANNE: When I say you're done, you can go back to the tables and read.
> MARCOS: Can we move our desks?
> ANNE: No, we need time to be quiet and think.

CELINA: I'm going to do a polim.
GEORGE: How do you do polims?
CLAUDIO: Mrs. Barry, when are you going to put up my polar bear poem?
(2/6/92)

As mentioned in Chapter 2, since classroom activities did not occur in any exact order over the course of the school day, there were seams (Manke, 1990) that provided openings for students to enter into negotiation with Anne regarding classroom process. The children in this excerpt were successful at receiving permission to "do journals," but Marcos's desire to move into small groups for this activity was denied. Two aspects of this negotiation are significant to a discussion of expertise as negotiated between students and teacher.

First, the students' agenda of journaling was not in conflict with the teacher's agenda of encouraging meaningful literacy activities. So students' enthusiasm and excitement for writing in their journals can be seen as a shared agenda of the teacher's. Thus, even though further negotiation occurred regarding how journaling would be done, the students and the teacher shared an agenda.

Second, Marcos's suggestion to move into small groups conflicted with Anne's agenda at that point. Her reason was given—"We need time to be quiet and think"—but she spoke for the group, using what Edwards and Mercer (1987) have noted as the "royal plural" (p. 131). Her own expertise as classroom boss went unquestioned here, as it usually did throughout the course of the school year when she did not want to take up student suggestions for classroom process. However, even though students did not often contest these kinds of classroom process decisions, they actively contested her knowledge claims if they had evidence to contradict them.

If we look again at the preceding transcription, the final three turns provide a fine illustration of how students publicly shared their expertise and contributed to building common knowledge. Celina indicates to the group her intention to use the journaling time to explore a particular genre of writing: poetry. George (one of the new students) asks Celina directly what a "polim" is. Claudio is able to interpret Celina's mispronunciation and rather than correct her overtly, he asks the teacher when his poem will be displayed on the bulletin board. He offers expertise as a writer of poetry to the group as an answer to George's question. Claudio can be seen as having triple expertise: understanding Celina's meaning when she says "polim," knowing what a poem is, and being a writer of poetry himself. Anne did not enter into this dialogue, instead sitting down to write in her own journal. The discussion ended there, and Claudio did not get an answer to his question.

In the next transcription, it can be seen how the process of negotiating journaling took a turn toward more student control (greater expertise and a larger handover of competence from teacher to students) by the end of the year. Furthermore, it provides an example of how the teacher worked to directly teach skills which support students' autonomy.

(1) CLAUDIO: Can we do our journals?

(2) ANNE: Are you anxious? (Within 10 seconds every child has her or his journal out and is starting to read or write.)

(3) FELIPE: What's the date today?

(4) ANNE: Oh, thank you, what is it?

(5) CHILD: Twenty-two

(6) ANNE: How do we write that? Where can you always check if you don't know?

(7) LATOYA: Calendar

(5/22/92)

Just as in the previous excerpt, journaling began with a student request to the teacher for permission to move into the activity. On this occasion, however, the students did not wait for permission from Anne but took out their journals and began rereading previous entries or started writing another. In fact, overt permission was never even granted but was only implicit in Anne's attention to Felipe's request for the date to be written on the board. So students' expertise by this point in the year had extended to implementing suggestions made by other students for classroom process—even without gaining explicit take-up by the teacher.

This sort of sharing of authority can be seen, then, as a gradual process, taking shape in a community of learners over a period of time. The small and subtle ways that teachers can work to scaffold students' expertise, rather than control it, can also be seen in Anne's comment to the class in turn 6. Rather than rely on the teacher remembering to write the date on the board each day, she implies, you can rely on yourself and use the calendar. She is helping Felipe to not need her expertise next time but to develop his own instead.

As this school year was Anne's first attempt at using journals in the classroom, she had many questions regarding how to do this most effectively. Many of these questions revolved around children's emergent writing, which she was considering in new ways based on the readings she had been doing (Calkins, 1986; Pappas, Kiefer, & Levstik, 1990; Routman, 1988, 1990). Issues of assessment, concern about students who continued for months to use prephonemic spelling or unsystematic letter stringing (Pappas et al., 1990), and the place of dictation all were ongoing topics of her discussions in the teachers' group as well as with me on my weekly visits. These issues, although important to Anne, are not addressed in this book; instead, in this chapter, I examine two topics that relate most closely to shared authority. The first of these are the ways in which journals changed, in part because of student initiations; and the second is Anne's concern regarding student-versus teacher-initiated writing.

JOURNALING: CHANGES IN GENRE

Anne, as she explained above, wrote in her own journal while students were writing in theirs and then sometimes read her entry to the class. These entries were reflections on the day, the activities of the class or school, or her life at home. Students' entries typically followed her pattern. However, as early as the third week of school, students began to write other genres in their journals. The first of these to appear was a write-up of a science experiment, which Melinda wrote after Anne had suggested the possibility to the class. Much more than any other child in the class, Melinda continued to use her journal throughout the year as a science log. As can be seen in Figure 7.2, she used the journal as a place to both record her observations and make predications. Although the teacher initiated the idea that journals could be used as science logs, not many students took up this invitation. This idea of offering invitations to students, rather than making specific assignments, is problematic for many teachers who are using such collaborative, interactive, dialogic forms of learning in their classrooms. Anne often wondered if it was enough to make the suggestion about using journals as science logs, or if

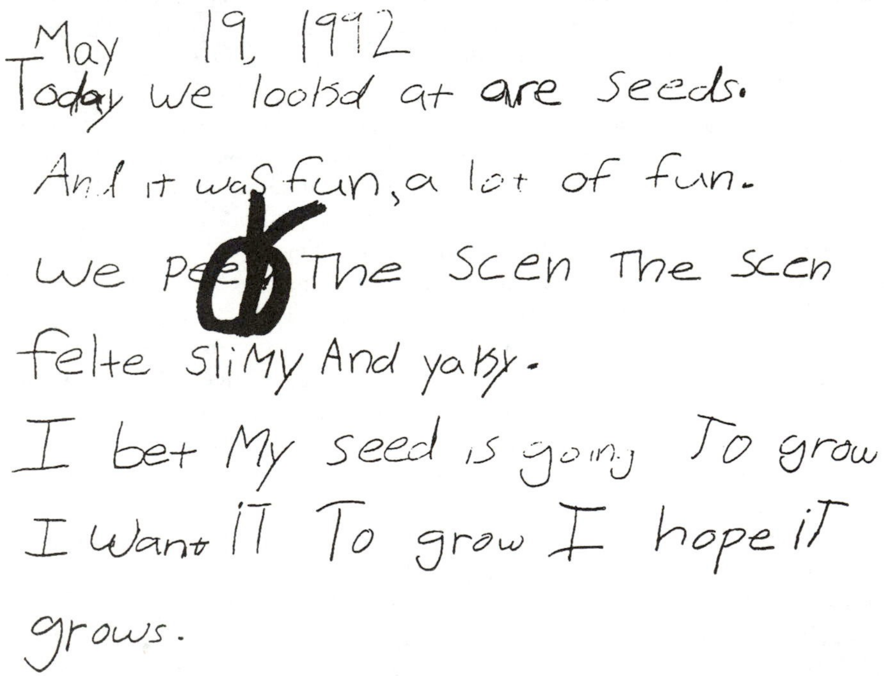

May 19, 1992
Today we looksd at are seeds.
And it was fun, a lot of fun.
We pd The Scen The Scen
felte sliMy And yaky.
I bet My seed is going To grow
I Want IT To grow I hope iT
grows.

FIGURE 7.2. Melinda's Science Log in Her Journal (with Seed Drawing)

there was more she should do to make this happen. Should she use her authority as teacher to insist that students' entries be a science log on a particular day? Or was it more important that the daily entry be on a topic that the student had selected themselves? These are the nitty-gritty questions of shared authority that come when teachers act on the belief that "knowledge itself is constructed by individuals as they make meaning of existential realities" (Stock & Robinson, 1989, p. 322). At what point does the teacher in a collaborative classroom *step in* and assign a particular genre of writing? This is the heart of what Anne grappled with regarding her students' writing throughout the year.

Another genre of writing that appeared early in students' journals was poetry; this is not surprising, since Anne copied numerous poems onto big chart paper and the class read them as a group almost daily. Additionally, each student had a book of collected poems that contained copies of the poems they had learned as a group. Furthermore, throughout the day Anne taught the class finger plays and chants with rhythmic and rhyming qualities. Much of the students' poetry had the same structure as the poems and chants they had learned as a group.

Anne's authority, then, in introducing the genre of poetry had a direct effect on the writing or authoring students did on their own. This is a central point in the discussion of shared authority and underscores the importance of examining the two dimensions of classroom authority. Sharing authority is not merely a process of offering students activity choices or input into classroom tasks. The content dimension of authority must also be noticed, since teacher authority shapes not only the curriculum materials and genres presented to students but also the very ways in which students interact with these and make them their own. As Lensmire (1994) points out, "Teacher-assigned genres and topics may not be limiting, but actually expand student chances for growth in writing" (p. 151). It is not enough merely to turn students loose to choose what and how to write. This is precisely the laissez-faire interpretation of writing workshops that Lisa Delpit (1988) criticizes; particularly for students from nonmainstream homes, teachers need actively to share their knowledge of cultural systems and ways of organizing knowledge (as well as invite students to bring their home culture systems to school, even if the teacher is not privy to them). These systems of the dominant culture must be intentionally taught and cannot be left to incidental learning.

Teacher- Versus Student-Initiated Writing

Anne experimented with ways to direct and control the development of students' use of multiple genres in writing. One way in which she encouraged students to continue writing poetry was to put their poems up on bulletin boards as well as display them in the hallways. She also used the beginning of journal-writing time to introduce different genres and prod students to experiment. For example, after she had finished reading *Charlotte's Web* (White, 1952) out loud to the class, Anne did a minilesson (Calkins, 1986) on how to write a character study. Using group-composed writing (see Chapter 8), the class first developed a list of characteristics about Mrs. Arable, the mother in *Charlotte's Web*. Then Anne used this list to compose a paragraph about the character. The following excerpt illustrates how Anne's introduction of this genre both invited and *compelled* students to write a character study of their own:

(Anne is at the board with the character checklist and character study from yesterday.)

(1)   ANNE: You've all had a break, you've all had a walk, you've all had a drink of water. That means you're set. Remember yesterday we made a character checklist? Let's read it. Start from the top.

(2)   (Children read character checklist out loud.)

(3)   ANNE: The next thing we did, what did I do?

(4)   MONTREL: Wrote about Mrs. Arable.

(5)   ANNE: I wrote about Mrs. Arable.

(6)   CELINA: That's what we're going to do—write about people? I'm going to write about Charlotte.

(7)   GUILLERMO: Write a poem?

(8)   ANNE: Pick a person from the book that you liked and tell about them.

(9)   RICKY: And draw a picture?

(10) ANNE: Yes, you can draw a picture.

(4/3/92)

Celina is a successful student, and as is the way with such students, she has grasped, in turn 6, that the teacher has modeled a writing process that she expects the students to use during their journal-writing time. Guillermo, too, understands that a specific genre of writing is being subtly requested here (turn 7), but he is confused and wonders if he's supposed to write a poem. This misunderstanding causes Anne to get more directive, and in turn 8 she spells out exactly what she wants the students to do. In this excerpt, then, Anne has moved past just mentioning other genres of writing and has modeled her process for writing a character study. Celina correctly understands this modeling to mean that the teacher expects students to write a character study of their own. This is a fascinating exchange that is quite useful in an analysis of teacher authority. The subtle but powerful role of teacher as demonstrator is not lost on the ever-observant Celina. Being successful in school certainly requires that the student figure out what the teacher wants; Celina has done that here. What could be missed in this exchange, however, is the benefit Anne derives from having a student such as Celina interpret her intentions to the class community. Celina in turn 6 is enthusiastic about the assigned writing: "That's what we're going to do—write about people? I'm going to write about Charlotte." Thus Celina's understanding of the project, acceptance of it, and enthusiasm for it work as a translation for other children who might not understand what to do. In this way, Celina's initiation worked to make Anne's job easier. (Of course, I should point out that Celina didn't always "buy into" Anne's projects. Outspoken students can also use the floor to challenge teacher authority and invite others to join them.) Celina is quite an authority in this exchange: mediating between the community of her peers and that of her teacher.

Anne experimented with this character study out of her ongoing concern regarding how much student writing should be teacher-initiated. In talking after school that day she said:

> Here's my big question—you know about the student initiations. I still think I'm too far to the student side. I think it has to be both somehow. . . . A first-grade teacher in my master's program did this really neat thing with describing buttons, and her kids did some amazing stuff. I'm going crazy with it. I'm not getting stuff that good from these kids. What am I getting? Is it right? . . . Yesterday I showed them the process of writing about characters and led them through the checklist. But I'm not getting really good stuff. (4/3/92)

After she visited another Chicago public school well known for its work in the area of writing, Anne reflected:

> I saw wonderful writing displayed all through the school, but what I saw on bulletin boards was not what I felt was student-initiated writing. A lot of it was, "Today I went on a walk and saw . . . " Or sentence starters: "Fortunately/Unfortunately . . . " (3/30/92)

Anne's concern about student versus teacher initiation in writing stemmed in large part from the conflict she felt regarding her new beliefs about the benefits of a process approach to writing and her disappointment when she compared her students' writing to that from other teachers' students: "I'm not getting really good stuff." Anne wanted to get "good stuff," but she also believed that students' writing needed to be sparked by authentic purpose and meaning.

One aspect that Anne did not question during the three years we worked on this project was the political significance of topic and theme choices—whether made by her or by the students. For instance, in the button writing assignment, Anne focused on the writing skills of the students, not on the vacuousness of such an assignment. But Anne did not get pushed to deal with this subject by the writings of her students, either. Many teachers report that they have dilemmas about how to respond to students' sexist, racist, classist, or violent pieces. Even the theme of cartoons, such as Ninja Turtles, can become a problem for the process-writing teacher. As Anne did not face this problem, this huge issue of teacher authority is not addressed here. (For excellent treatments of this topic, see Davies, 1993; Gilbert, 1991; Lensmire, 1994; Willinsky, 1990.)

Anne, in her concern about student versus teacher initiation in writing, can be seen as dealing with the power issues inherent in teaching. Even when teachers make the move toward a process approach in writing, they are not free from issues of authority and control. The very fact that the teacher is insisting that students formulate their own topics and develop authentic reasons to write can be seen as a powerful, authoritative move by the teacher. Willinsky (1990), in discussing process writing, advises against embracing a utopian vision of the workshop-style classroom that denies the power of the teacher:

> Students busily taken up with publishing projects in the workshop setting seem to have dissolved any questions about power and authority in the classroom, questions that tend to disrupt other classrooms at times. . . . The power which makes this space a classroom rather than coffee shop is still present but the teacher has found a way to circulate it through all the participants rather than lord it over them. (p. 52)

This serves to remind us that classroom power and authority do not disappear with restructured pedagogies such as journal writing. Rather, as Willinsky so clearly says, the power is circulated in different ways. This is a very Foucauldian notion (see Chapter 2) pointing to how power is not a possession, but rather is negotiated and reformulated in the discourses of social actors. Hence the very act of requiring authenticity, requiring students to choose what to write, is not necessarily an "empowering" pedagogy, but can also be seen as powerful, and could even turn out to be oppressive.

Learning New Genres

In questioning her role of director of student writing, Anne is bringing this power issue to the forefront and pondering ways to encourage students to develop autonomy and at the same time push them to learn new genres of writing. Just how much should she insist on? Anne poses these questions not only theoretically, but from the day-to-day perspective of a classroom teacher who must plan and execute the students' day. For example, she wondered a year later:

> I grapple with this, should I have a pile of lit logs and a pile of science logs and a pile of poetry books? Do I pick the science logs up on a certain day and say, "Today, I'd really like you to write and respond to seeds?" (5/31/93)

During the year of this study, the students *did* respond to their science experiments with seeds; yet the openness of Anne's structure allowed for them to show this response using a variety of genres.

Figure 7.3 shows Maya's journal entry. She told Anne it said: "My seeds are growing. The teacher is proud of me. I love my seeds. Seeds are great and I'm taking care of it. They need sun and water and soil." Here she is able to demonstrate her scientific understanding of what seeds need to grow as well as relate her feelings of success and pleasure.

Felipe, on the other hand, wrote a poem based on the structure of a poem the class had learned earlier (and similar in structure to his penguin poem, discussed in Chapter 5). Felipe's poem is shown in Figure 7.4; he explained it to Anne as follows:

5 little seeds, jumping around,
The first little seed fell down and cracked.
The second seed ran down and grew.
How can a silly seed do that silly thing?
And the third seed said, "Oh no, I'm growing."
The fourth seed said, "Hurray, I grew!"
And the fifth seed said, "This is good. Hurray, I'm yellow!"

In Felipe's poem he is able to weave in his understanding that seed growth begins with the seed hull cracking. He also shows his knowledge that this is not exactly a scientific treatment he is giving the topic: "How can a silly seed do that silly thing?" Contrast this poem of Felipe's with Melinda's more scientific observations and predications recorded in her journal (see Figure 7.2).

By introducing a variety of writing genres to the class and suggesting that students respond to their science experiment in their journals, Anne left the students plenty of room to define what genre they would use. This seems to be critical to sharing authority with students to author their own texts; that is, students must have the knowledge of a variety of written genres to truly share authority with the teacher for deciding exactly which genre they will use to respond. For without the more expert knowledge of the teacher regarding writing genres, students do not really have a choice at all. It is only *with* an understanding of the range of possibilities that exist that students can be seen as making informed choices. The greater the range of possibilities to which they have been exposed, the greater are the students' choices of how they will express their knowledge, understandings, thoughts, beliefs, ideas, and dreams; it is in the articulation of these that a power to act exists. For, as Pagano (1990) has so eloquently, noted:

Those who are prevented from speaking, those who are excluded from language, those whom Freire refers to as members of the "culture of silence," are deprived of the power to act on the world. They are deprived of authority. They are deprived of the power to inscribe their lives in the world. They are robbed of their histories and their bodies. (p. 139)

May 19,1992

My saes are •gonen
                 growing

The Teacher is per   of me
                  proud

I Love My saes
              secus

saes are goT
           great

and Im Tosh kcnT Of IT
       tahing

Ia ned Sun and
They

Wotr and SoL
             soil.

FIGURE 7.3. Maya's Journal Entry

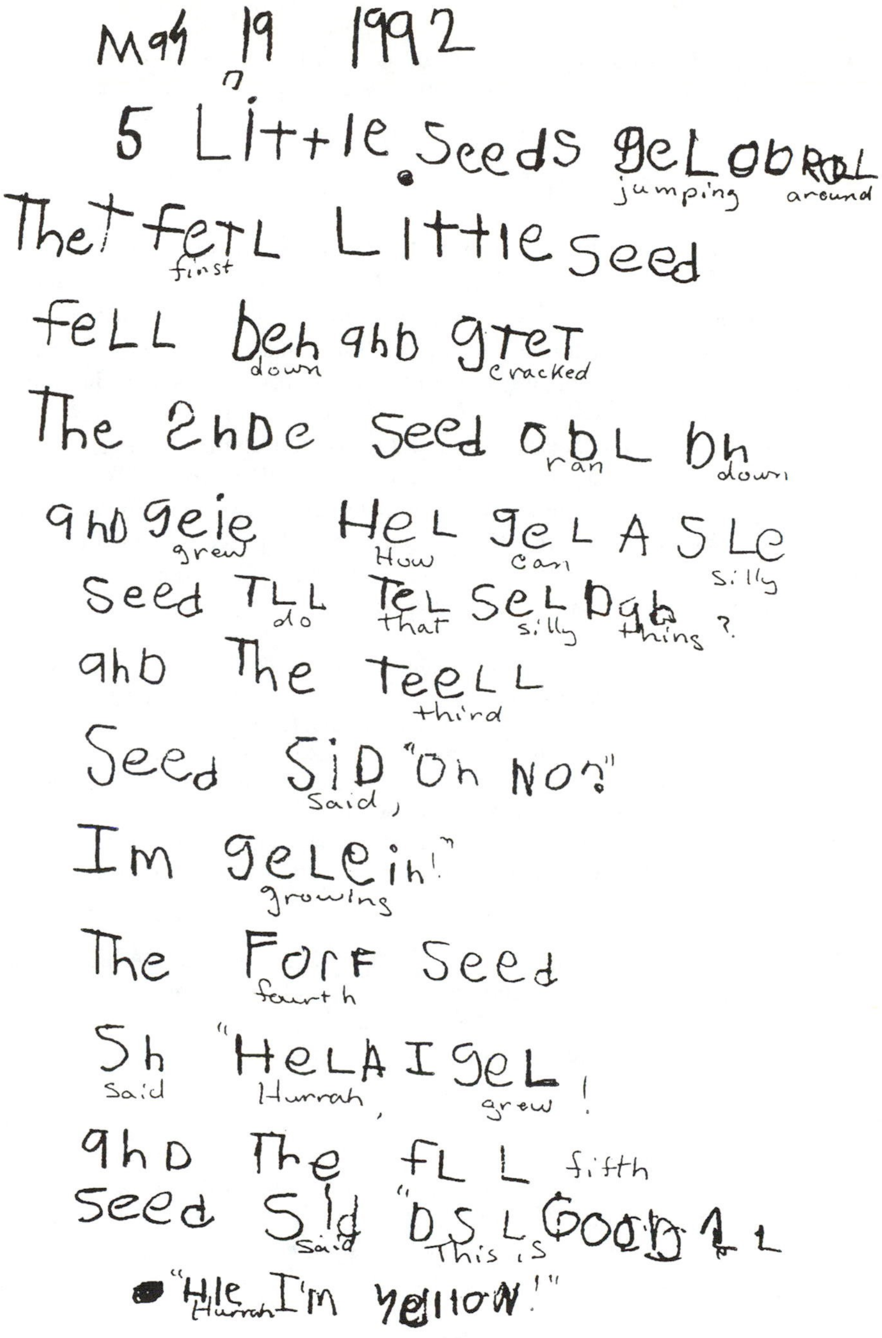

May 19 1992

5 Little Seeds geLobrol
jumping around

Thet fетL Little seed
first

fell beh ahb gтет
down   cracked

The εhbe seed o.bL bh
ran   down

ahb geie   HeL geL A S Le
grew   How can   silly

seed TLL TeL SeL Dgh ?
do   that   silly thing

ahb The TeeLL
third

Seed SiD "Oh NO?"
said,

Im geLein!"
growing

The ForF Seed
fourth

Sh "HeLA I geL !
Said   Hurrah,   grew

ahb The fLL fifth
seed SLd "D.S L Goog ↑L
Said This is

"Hle I'm yellow!"
Hurrah

FIGURE 7.4. Felipe's Journal Entry

And conversely, by becoming the authors of their own texts, students are encouraged to speak, to act, and to do these boldly and with authority.

JOURNALING: A SOCIAL PROCESS

One of the main changes Anne and the students made during the year in the routine of journaling was its movement from a solitary activity to a social one. In the beginning of the year, while they were journaling, students' desks were in the long-row format, with aisles separating each student on both sides. Students were expected to write without talking or getting out of their seats. For instance, in Chapter 3 there is a description of the elaborate pantomime rituals two students went through to negotiate for an eraser without talking or getting up. However, by the middle of the year, journal writing was taking place with students' desks in the small-group formation used during math, shared reading, and other group activities. Thus journaling moved from being a quiet activity to one in which exploratory talk was not only permitted but was seen by Anne as a component of the writing process itself. As Barnes (1990) explains:

> When children discuss a topic without an authoritative adult their talk is typically *exploratory*—hesitant, often incomplete, hypothetical, directed not to making confident assertions but to exploring the range of possible accounts and explanations. The support of other members of the group seems to be crucial in this, especially the implicit support that comes from taking up one another's ideas and developing them. Exploratory talk seems to . . . [bring] together old knowledge and new experiences . . . so that they modify one another. . . . Exploratory talk serves the purposes of understanding, giving the pupils an opportunity to reorder their pictures of the world in relation to new ideas and new experiences. (p. 73)

In thinking back on the major changes she made in her teaching, Anne credits listening to students' exploratory talk as a significant turning point for her. The year before this study, as part of an action-research project for university credit, Anne recorded small-group discussion. She spoke about how this influenced her thinking:

> I had Easter and spring pictures, so it was a lot of my initiation—more didactic, but it was to see what the talk was. In retrospect it showed me how social learning is and how talk reflects that. Looking back on it now, that was my big shift—just listening to how much came out of the children talking to each other. (5/31/93)

Next she became increasingly aware of how enthusiastic her students were about sharing their writing informally with one another. In November of the year of the classroom portion of this study, when she hadn't yet made the change to small-group journal writing, she told the teachers' group about this excitement: "The thing was the feeling in the room after they finished their writing and Montrel was jumping around and I told him to go read it to someone else and then everyone wanted to do that too" (11/18/91). By December, though, small-group sharing of journal writing had become a normal routine:

(Children are at separate desks, back from bathroom break.)

ANNE: Maybe you'd like to work in small groups for your journals today.
CHILDREN: (In unison) Yes!

(Students move their desks into small groups without anything more being said by Anne. They start talking to each other about their writings and drawings.)

(12/16/91)

This chance to engage in exploratory talk about their journal entries, to read one another's writing and examine one another's illustrations, was a process in which students happily engaged. Children quite eagerly took full advantage of the opportunity to share their journals with their tablemates. In fact, by February, students were circulating to different small groups than the ones to which they had been assigned by the teacher.

Such movement and talk, however exciting for the young writers, proved to be more work for Anne to manage than had quiet journal writing at separate desks. Children had much more autonomy to borrow crayons, markers, or erasers, or even look around the room for words they wanted to use in their writing. All this movement and conversation occurred at the same time Anne held individual conferences with each student on her or his writing. To add to the bustle, by January Anne was allowing students to move directly from journal writing into shared reading without first waiting to conference with her. Thus the process of journaling had moved from being done in silent, solitary rows to small groups with flexibility to change not only location in the room but between activities as well.

Anne talked about the problems she faced in allowing the children so much autonomy and about how she talked individually to the students who did not seem to be writing:

I have to tell them sometimes, "You're not doing what you're supposed to be doing." Like Adrian, I went up to him and said, "How much have you gotten written?" He and a few others just sit and talk too much. It's really gotten to be a problem. (5/4/92)

Sometimes Anne would pull in the reins to the whole class—as when she said: "Get down to business. Decide where you're going to be and stay there. Don't move" (4/3/92).

This raises the inherent dilemma for teachers who believe that exploratory talk is a valuable component of classroom learning. How can the teacher possibly manage so much activity and talk and still know whether students are doing what the teacher thinks they are supposed to be doing? This is one place in which sharing authority becomes problematic. The teacher is responsible for maintaining an atmosphere that she or he thinks is conducive to learning. The obvious problem is how to monitor all this activity and track students' individual progress and growth. As discussed in Chapter 6, Anne struggled to find ways to do this most effectively. However, as much as management issues are a huge concern to many teachers— particularly less experienced teachers—what is raised here is a thornier and deeper problem with sharing authority. And that is: At what point were students really even sharing authority for the work of the classroom? After all, when students were not complying with Anne's desire that they write—as with Adrian in the above quote— she imposed her order and her will. When enough people in the class seemed "off task," Anne resorted to a directive that all students "not move." So can a sharing of authority even exist in a classroom? When the teacher has this much power and responsibility, are chances for student autonomy and exploratory, collaborative talk and learning just covert ways to get the students to fulfill the teacher's agenda?

Surely elements of teachers' desire for control exist even when they create classroom environments in which students have some choices and get to make some decisions. As Mary Manke (1993) noted regarding a teacher in one of her studies:

> [The teacher] remarked that she regularly offered choices to students in the area of learning, but these were always choices between two things that were desirable from her point of view, and she said she believed that students learn better when they have the opportunity to choose. (p. 25)

Therefore, in critically examining shared authority, it is important to consider *whose agenda is being fulfilled* and what opportunities exist for students to enter into setting their own agendas. When students are able to initiate and negotiate for *what will count* as classroom work, they are truly sharing authority with the teacher. The development of at-home journals indicates that such a sharing sometimes took place in this classroom.

AT-HOME JOURNALS

In November, Melinda proposed that students be given separate notebooks so they could write journals at home as well as school. Thus a new activity—at-home journals—was created. Anne gave each student who requested it a spiral note-book in which to write at home. By the second week, over half the class had one. Throughout the year, students brought their at-home journals to school to read out loud to the class. These journals were treasured and cared for: Many of the families did not have extra money for school supplies, so a new notebook was a special object. (I think a lot of middle-class people don't realize how precious school supplies can be for poor children. When I lived in Chicago, I routinely gave Halloween trick-or-treaters a choice between candy or a brand-new unsharpened pencil. I gave away hundreds of pencils every year; children could be heard shout-ing up and down the street, "Hey, she's givin' out pencils down there!")

The creation of at-home journals was clearly a student initiation and indicates a sharing of authority for both dimensions of authority: the process dimension of how work is implemented and the content dimension of what will count as knowl-edge. Furthermore, the genesis of this new activity illustrates the notion that a sharing of authority has at its very root a sharing of agendas. For one of children's agendas in a literate society is to join that society and become literate also. It reaches further than that, though; as Lucy Calkins (1986) has noted: "Human beings have a deep need to represent their experience through writing. We need to make our truths beautiful" (p. 3). So these children in Room 104, in clamoring for at-home journals, must be seen as creating a mutual agenda with their teacher: Their de-sire for literacy fits with her agenda for them. It is, as I have said before, a mutu-ally constructed agenda. It is this mutual agenda, I argue, from which a sharing of authority can best exist.

EDITING AND REVISING

No discussion of sharing authority during journal writing in Anne Barry's class would be complete without examining the process of editing and revising that took place as students wrote. As depicted in Figures 7.1, 7.3, and 7.4, Anne wrote con-ventional spellings underneath students' initial journal entries. She circulated from desk to desk and had students read to her what was written. They talked briefly about the content of the piece, and Anne suggested ways they could elaborate or expand on what had been written. She also used this time to point out ways to make the message clearer by adding words or changing punctuation. For example:

(Students are in small groups writing drafts of chapter books. George reads me his version of "Beauty and the Beast." Anne comes over.)

ANNE: Good, keep going. Who said that? Read that to me (pointing to a sentence).
GEORGE: I LOVE YOU.

ANNE: Did somebody say that? Who said that?
GEORGE: The girl!
ANNE: Well, "said the girl" maybe. Say that—the girl said, "I love you."
   Because we have to know that. The reader has to know. Good job, super.
   (Anne walks away.)
GEORGE: (Reads his pages to Camila)
CAMILA: (To George) Remember to write—"the girl said"—the reader gots
   to know.

                                                                    (2/27/92)

So even the process of editing and revising became a social process in which students helped one another learn to write in ways that readers can understand. This
emphasis on writing in ways that the reader can understand is part of the constant
revision that is inherent when writers read back what they have written. Thus the
opportunity to get direct and individual teacher attention and support for writing
on almost a daily basis from Anne led students to help peers with their revisions
as well as to start editing their own pieces when they conferenced with the teacher:

(Camila is conferencing with Anne. She is reading her journal.)

CAMILA: No, that's not what I meant. Not *for* me. I want it to be *to* me.
ANNE: Okay, good, change it.

                                                                    (1/22/92)

With the support of the teacher, students were able to revise their own work and
speak as *authorities* on their own writing. But the teacher had expertise to offer as
a writer and was able to teach students the art of communicating through writing.
So even as Anne allowed students to speak as authorities on their own texts, she
did not deny her expertise as a writer and a reader. Rather, she used this expertise
to nudge the students into honing their own skills and becoming skillful writers,
too. In classrooms in which the pedagogy is built around more collaborative, dialogic, and co-constructed forms of learning, teachers do not abdicate their authority
at all. Rather they are in an important position to share their knowledge, or authority, with students even as they help them develop their own strong voices and
communicate this authority in writing.

   In individual writing, which in Anne's class was called "Journals," students
shared authority primarily by being the authors of their own words and meanings.
This is so well reflected in Camila's quote used as the chapter title: "That's not
what I meant." In this way, students can be seen as actively engaged in creating
texts that represent their understandings of their lives and their world. The teacher's
critical balancing act is being able to share enough and prod enough to both challenge and support this effort to have the children's written texts tell their own stories.

8

"Some Men Make Dinner"

Discourse and Authority
in Teacher-Led Group Writing

An important routine in Anne Barry's first grade was teacher-led group-composed writing. Anne saw this teacher-led activity as a time to teach students the composing process, call attention to graphic-phonemic patterns (and other medium—or mechanical—aspects of writing), as well as create common texts that she then published as Big Books or on chart paper. This chapter addresses the ways in which authority was shared during group composing, looking particularly at the roles students played in initiating and the ways in which the teacher facilitated, controlled, and directed the process. Inherent in the group-composition process were negotiations regarding understandings and interpretations of the world; this is reflected in the chapter title excerpt—"Some men make dinner"—which occurred during a debate between a girl and a boy about whether men can indeed cook dinner for their children. Specifically examined are three different discourse patterns and the ways in which each of these left differing degrees of control for teacher and students. The first pattern is one that is characterized by many opportunities for student initiation, cross-discussion, and peer evaluation. The second pattern is that of teacher transmission of specific information. The third is called "cued elicitation" (Edwards, D., & Mercer, 1987) and is characterized by the teacher leading students through a series of questions to arrive at specific understandings.

GROUP-COMPOSED WRITING

As Pappas and colleagues (1995) explain, teacher-led group-composed writing

> works well with younger children because the teacher takes over some of the mechanical aspects so that children can concentrate on the content. . . . It enables the teacher to demonstrate the thinking process involved in getting ideas into print and to make explicit the kinds of choices writers face—choices of voice, purpose, and form, as well as the medium aspects involved in creating a finished piece of writing. (p. 255)

Anne began to use this process in September when the class had finished reading *Excuses, Excuses* (Butler, 1984). Anne told the teachers' group how this first group writing came about:

> We did a Big Book. And again, it was spontaneous. We had read the book *Excuses, Excuses.* . . . It had stuff like, "I'm sorry I'm late, my . . . " Well they loved it *so* much, and they were just yelling by the end of the book, "Excuses, excuses." So I asked them, would you like to write this up? And each child had a turn, "I'm sorry I'm late," and to say what their excuse was. Mr. Lopez [the principal] walked in, he must have heard us yelling or something, so they put him in the book. For some children who aren't very vocal, it was a great experience. They saw the others doing it and they got the pattern. So I guess my comment about language is, it was a moment when it just happened. It seems like I have a lot of those moments. (9/23/91)

The class later published the book: Each student illustrated her or his own page, and Anne glued the pages into a blank Big Book she had bought. This book remained a favorite text throughout the year during shared reading time.

STUDENT-INITIATED DISCOURSE PATTERN

The evolution of the students' group-authored book illustrates how a sharing of authority is an interactive process between teacher and students. Anne called the writing "spontaneous," by which she means she had not planned it. In other words, she did not set out to lead the class in a group writing of their own version of *Excuses, Excuses*. However, by being willing to follow the enthusiasm of the students and having the *expertise* to suggest a specific format, Anne was able to share her authority for both classroom process and knowledge. That is, students' interests were being followed to determine what the work of the class was, their ideas were creating a group text, and Anne's expertise as teacher was being used to further this process.

As students experienced success in group-composed writing, it fostered more and more initiations from students to continue this co-authoring. Excited by the accomplishment of the first group book, Anne began to build in weekly teacher-led writing. She introduced a variety of genres of writing, all involving contributions from each member of the class. A week before Thanksgiving, for instance, the class wrote the directions for cooking a turkey. On Monday, when the students came back to school, Anne had copied the turkey cooking directions onto chart paper and posted it on the magnetized chalkboard. What follows is a transcription of what happened when the students saw their published piece. Notice the ways in which authority was shared in revising the text as well as planning classroom process:

(Students begin filing into the classroom from library.)

(1)   CHILD 1: What's that? (pointing to turkey cooking directions)
(2)   CHILDREN: (Starting to spontaneously read in unison) YOU BUY THE
        TURKEY AT THE STORE. (Anne gets long pointer and starts pointing to
        the words as students read.) THEN YOU TAKE IT HOME AND THEN YOU
        WASH YOUR HANDS AND YOU WASH THE TURKEY. YOU PUT IT TO DRY. THEN
        YOU PUT THE FILLING AND STUFFING INSIDE THE TURKEY. YOU PUT OIL ON
        THE TURKEY. YOU PUT HIM IN THE OVEN. THEN TURN THE OVEN ON. AND
        PUT IT ON 20 DEGREES FOR ONE HOUR. YOU WAIT TILL IT COOKS. YOU CALL
        THE FAMILY AND YOU SAY, "THANK YOU GOD FOR THE FOOD."
(3)   MONTREL: What about and then you eat. (Everyone laughs.)
(4)   ANNE: Did we forget to add that?
(5)   CHILDREN: (In unison) Yeah.
(6)   ANNE: I'm so proud of you, you know why. You haven't had the
        chance to read that since Friday. Now todaaaaay, we're going to do
        something really exciting. You're going to tell me—think about
        it—what you're going to stuff your turkey with.
(7)   CLAUDIO: Stuffing.
(8)   ANNE: Don't tell, it's a secret you're thinking about it. And then we'll
        put it on the board, there's enough space for everyone to tell me.
        Let me get my blue pen and . . what were we going to add to it?
        (Lots of children talking and offering answers all at once)
(9)   ANNE: Then you cut it up?
(10) CLAUDIO: Then you cut it and then you eat it.
(11) MIRIAM: We already have that.
(12) CLAUDIO: Oh . . then you serve the family. (Anne starts to write and
        children read in unison as she writes.)
(13) CHILDREN: (Reading) THEN. YOU. CUT. IT. UP.
(14) ANNE: All right, I've added this, Claudio.
(15) CHILDREN: (In unison) THEN YOU CUT IT UP AND THEN YOU EAT IT UP.
        (Anne writes complete sentence on the board.)
(16) ANNE: Is that all? Is that what you want?
(17) CHILDREN: AND THEN YOU EAT IT UP.
(18) ANNE: OK, you want to read the last lines? (Children read it again.)
(19) CELINA: Can I read this? (She is holding her journal.)
(20) ANNE: Is that your home journal?
(21) CELINA: Yes
(22) SILVIA: Can we do journals?
(23) CHILDREN: (Many, chanting) Let's do journals. (Anne gestures with
        her hand for Celina to come up and read her journal.)

                                                        (11/25/91)

This excerpt illustrates the way in which Anne followed student initiations for both rereading the text and revising it. The students, in fact, began reading the turkey-cooking directions without teacher direction (turn 2). Anne used this opportunity to grab the long pointer and facilitate their spontaneous group reading by keeping them all together. This also provided support for students who were not yet making strong connections between the printed and spoken word. Montrel, in turn 3, suggests a revision, which Anne begins to take up in turn 8. She marks her intention to take their suggestions by getting the blue pen she used in the published draft. Furthermore, Anne indicates that rather than simply use Montrel's turn as a revision, she is opening up the process to the entire class: "What were *we* going to add to it?" This can be seen as underscoring the fact that this is a group-composed text, open to negotiation.

Miriam's comment to Claudio in turn 11 ("We already have that") shows that this negotiation is one in which students can directly address each other; they do not have to go through the teacher as facilitator. As was seen during other group activities of child- and teacher-led read-alouds, cross-discussion (Lemke, 1990) is a part of the normal discourse pattern in this classroom. Claudio takes Miriam's feedback seriously (turn 12) and changes his contribution. Anne, however, ignores Miriam's comment, either because she didn't hear it or because she knows she is wrong. The opportunity to engage in peer cross-discussion, whether taken up by the teacher or not, is an essential reflection of a sharing of discourse opportunities and, thereby, authority. It serves cognitive purposes as well:

> The child also has a contribution to make, stemming from his [sic] own interests and directed by his own purpose. The sort of interaction that will be most beneficial for his development, therefore, is that which gives due weight to the contribution of both parties and emphasizes mutuality and reciprocity in the meanings that are constructed and negotiated through talk. (Wells, 1981, p. 115)

Anne's talk in this excerpt clearly reinforces the "mutuality and reciprocity" of the meanings of the students, checking and rechecking (turns 16 and 18) that the group text is agreed upon and understood.

As well as illustrating the opportunities for students to co-author texts during group-composed writing, this excerpt also portrays another important aspect of shared authority. If the floor is genuinely open to student direction and authority is shared for some aspects of classroom process, the teacher will not always follow her or his own plans. It is obvious in the transcription above that Anne comes to the chalkboard with a specific agenda (see turn 6). Her plan is to build upon the turkey-cooking directions with a recipe for stuffing. What happens, though, is that the class revises the previous day's writing and then Celina proposes she read her journal to the class (turn 19). Students take up Celina's suggestion, creating a groundswell of vocal support for moving from group-composed writing to child-led journal read-alouds. Anne tables her own agenda for writing a stuffing recipe and follows the students' lead into journals. Thus students were actively sharing authority with the teacher for deciding classroom process (who gets to do what, where, when, and how).

This interaction should be seen as a negotiation in which the teacher was the ultimate arbiter of what would happen next. The fact that Anne did indeed take up Celina's suggestion served to legitimate this type of request and encourage student initiation. Anne seemed almost delighted when discussing these events, usually chuckling about how assertive her students were. During group composing, this style of directing classroom process had its counterpart in the authors' assertiveness regarding what it was they wanted to say. Here, too, Anne followed their lead; as Anne recounted to the teachers' group:

We were reading the poem "Jelly on the Plate" (Booth, Booth, Pauli, & Phenix, 1984), and there was lots of wiggling from loose teeth in the room, and I said, "Let's write a poem about wiggling." And I said, "Let's start with loose teeth." And they *demanded* it read tooth, not teeth. They insisted. (3/23/92)

Student Evaluation

Throughout the year during this group-composed writing, students continued to take their words and meanings earnestly. They listened to each other's comments and discussed the ideas with utter seriousness. This is well illustrated in the next excerpt, when students had just finished choral reading the May poem from *Chicken Soup with Rice* (Sendak, 1962). This excerpt is an excellent example of a discourse pattern in which the floor is open to student initiations and teacher control is directed toward channeling these initiations.

(1) ANNE: Should we write a recipe called/
(2) CLAUDIO: Robin soup! (Anne starts writing students' suggestions on the board: "2 insects; 3 worms; 4 butterflies.")
(3) CHILD 1: Five rattlesnakes!
(4) CHILD 2: How can a robin eat rattlesnakes?
(5) MARCOS: Five robins!
(6) HENRY: (Turning to Marcos) He's not going to put his own friends in there, is he?
(7) GUILLERMO: Five worms.
(8) ANNE: We already have three worms. What do you think, should we add the five and we'd get . . .
(9) CHILD 3: We'd get eight.
(10) CHILD 4: Or 38. If you put the three and the five next to each other.

(11) ANNE: Right, it would be 38 if we made it 3 tens and 8 ones. Well, what do you think? Who put the worms up here?

(12) MONTREL: Adrian.

(13) ANNE: Adrian, would it be OK with you if we added some more, since you were the author of that? (Adrian nods his assent.)

(14) GUILLERMO: Then it will be eight worms.

(15) ANNE: Is eight worms OK? OK, we'll add that. (Children continue to add ingredients, with Anne calling on students so that everyone who wants a turn gets one.)

(16) ANNE: Now we can stop adding to the soup and say what we are going to do with all these things.

(17) CELINA: Cut 'em and mix 'em up.

(18) ANNE: Should we say that? Let's read what we have. (Class reads ingredients together with Anne's help.)

(19) ANNE: What are we going to do with all these? These are called the ingredients. . . . What are we going to do?

(20) CELINA: Cut 'em and mix 'em.

(21) ANNE: Let me get this down. (They take turns, and with Anne's questioning, dictate: First you cut the insects and the rest of the ingredients. Then get a bowl, put some water in the bowl. Mix the ingredients all together.)

(22) ANNE: Is that it? . . . Camila?

(23) CAMILA: He's cooking a meal for his babies.

(24) CLAUDIO: It's for dinner.

(25) ANNE: (Writing) OK, the robin . is making . . dinner for his/

(26) LATOYA: Kids

(27) CELINA: And his wife.

(28) MONTREL: Noooo. Because girls make dinner, not men.

(29) MAYA: Men can cook.

(30) CELINA: Yeah, some men make dinner.

(31) ANNE: Yeah, some men make dinner and some women. I'll put: The robin is making dinner for his kids.

(5/5/92)

This transcript provides multiple examples of students negotiating the content of the group-composed recipe. The teacher has shared her control of classroom knowledge by opening the floor to this co-construction of meaning. Anne has, in Newman's (1991) words, created "contexts which allow learners to make sense of the world collaboratively" (p. 112). The students listen to one another's contributions and evaluate them based on their own understandings. For example, in turns 4 and 6, students challenge one another regarding the sense of putting rattlesnakes and robins into the soup. They speak directly to each other, without channeling their evaluations through the teacher. This evidence of student evaluation of content demonstrates that the traditional IRE classroom discourse pattern has been displaced. By students sharing authority with the teacher for checking and evaluating peer comments, they are sharing in the process of establishing a shared understanding, which is described this way by Edwards, D., and Mercer (1987):

> There are some basic elements of the process of establishing a shared understanding, of building an ever-expanding foundation of shared knowledge which will carry the weight of future discourse. These are the offering of new information, reference to existing past experience, requests for information, and *tests or 'checks' on the validity of interpretation of information offered.* (p. 6; emphasis added)

In this way, then, peer feedback during group-composed writing worked to contribute to an ever-expanding body of "common knowledge" (Edwards, D., & Mercer, 1987) that the class not only held together but had actually constructed together. Part of this common knowledge was written in the pieces that the class co-authored. And these books, poems, recipes, and stories became common texts that students read together throughout the year.

Teacher Authority with Student Evaluations

Teachers are not invisible in the development of common knowledge, and in sharing their authority, they have not abdicated it. There were times within this type of student evaluation that the teacher used her authority to intercede. Returning to the previous transcript, turns 23 through 31 provide an excellent example of this. Montrel's understanding of the gender division of labor is challenged by both Maya and Celina. Anne sides with the girls' version and reinforces this by promptly writing the sentence. At this point, she does not leave the floor open to discussion or let the students work out a consensus on what they believe. Negotiating about the number of worms that go into robin soup is one thing—reinforcing the knowledge that men can cook is something else. Portrayed here, then, is a place in the process of group-composed writing where the teacher clearly asserts her authority—speaking as an expert and not negotiating knowledge with her students. Teachers often grapple with how much to assert their authority when dealing with issues such as sexism and racism—particularly when they are sensitive to competing with students' home cultures. I am reminded of a very experienced teacher I heard speak at a conference on teacher research; her inquiry concerned children's ideas of gender and exclusion/inclusion in group activities. After 20 years of teaching, she had decided she was going to step in and assert that it was not okay with her for students to exclude girls from the ball field or boys from the cooking area. This teacher's struggle illustrates so well the tension many teachers feel in asserting their values and using their authority to shape the discourses and behaviors in their classrooms. In large part because of the individualism of the mainstream culture, many teachers attempt to stay "neutral" and try not to "impose" their beliefs about such matters as gender equity on their students. However, by not stepping in and addressing the issue, a value *is* being communicated: it is all right to exclude people based on gender. Of course, even in the claiming of authority through intervention, teachers have moment-to-moment choices regarding strategy: Should they intervene, as Anne did in the above excerpt, and unilaterally *declare* that men can make dinner? Should they have a class discussion that explores the topic? Should they follow up this topic the next day with a read-aloud about women and men in nontraditional roles? Should they invite a classroom father in to do a cooking project? The questions about how to assert teacher authority in pushing agendas of equity are lengthy, weighty, and important.

DIRECT TRANSMISSION

Anne also spoke as an authority on the art of writing, sharing her own process and teaching specific skills almost every time she led a group composition. What follows is an example of the second discourse pattern discussed in this chapter, that of direct transmission by teacher. At one point in the creation of "robin soup," her lesson sounded like this:

> CHILD 1: Erase it.
> ANNE: I can erase it. Usually, when I write, this is what I do when I want to add something. I put a little arrow and I put the word that I want up there. I'm not ready to publish it yet. We're rewriting it—we're checking it. That's why when you write you reread things—making sure that it sounds right, that it reads right.
>
> (5/5/92)

Thus, in the collaborative classroom in which teachers make room for student initiations, peer discussion, and a co-construction of meaning, there is also room for transmission, or didactic, teaching. Anne did not wait for students to discover ways to mark their texts for editing or revising, she *directly taught* a way that worked for her. It should be noticed, however, that this transmission of information—much like her introduction of the word *ingredients* (see turn 19 of the second transcript in this chapter, on making robin soup)—was an explicit response to something that had come from the students. As explained by Pappas and colleagues (1995):

> The fact that teachers respect and encourage children's inquiry . . . does not mean that teachers have a laissez-faire attitude in teaching or that they never share their expertise

and knowledge with their students or never directly tell their students some information on a topic that students may want or need. (p. 44)

Therefore it is important to keep in mind that teachers sharing authority with students so that the students can become authors and authorities in their own right does not mean that they deny *their* authority. In fact, teachers must share their understandings directly with students *in order to share their own authority*. To do otherwise would not be sharing authority but withdrawing or abdicating it. Accordingly, one of the puzzles for teachers who seek to share power and control is deciding when to share their knowledge as teachers and when to make room for students to negotiate their own understandings. A way to navigate this puzzle is to think of teachers' input as contingently responsive (Wells & Chang-Wells, 1992) to students' initiatives. In that way, teachers carefully listen to students' understandings and provide a bridge between the students' knowledge and the teacher's. Thus "becoming literate is best seen in terms of an apprenticeship, in which the learner is inducted into the model of literacy implicitly held by the more expert performer" (Wells & Chang-Wells, 1992, p. 147). It is at precisely this point that poor, urban children of color and their teachers sometimes miss each other. For teachers to be contingently responsive to student initiatives, they must be able to make the link between their own understandings and culture and the child's understandings and cultures. If they are different, this requires a process of translation that must be preceded by understanding and appreciation. For children from nonmainstream homes to be apprenticed to the literacy forms of the culture of power (Delpit, 1988), teachers must be able to serve as the bridge.

Many of Anne's more didactic teaching moments during teacher-led group-composed writing related to the procedure of rereading and revising—a process she wanted to model in an attempt to encourage students to use it in their own journal writing. This became more and more frequent as the year progressed. As Anne explained: "From reading the Routman [1990] book I'm thinking about how she uses demonstration of her writing to make metacognitive to kids all the steps she goes through in revising. I need to do that more" (12/16/91). For example, while co-writing a book about their trip to the zoo, Anne explained to the class:

> Sometimes when you write, you only write a couple sentences, and you go back, and you reread so you know what you have. So you don't repeat the same thing. Now, we're back up here. Let's look. (*They re-read*) And I forgot . . a punctuation mark on the end. That's a telling sentence, and I give it a period. Very nice. (4/10/92)

With this encouragement to see writing as able to be edited and revised, students began to initiate changes of their own and became editors of their teacher's writing. The following excerpt shows an example of this during group-composed writing:

CAMILA: You forgot the *s* [in *birds*].
ANNE: I forgot the *s*. Camila, that's *wonderful*. Should I go back?
CHILDREN: Yes
ANNE: When you reread, do you correct?
CHILDREN: Yes
ANNE: Yes. I made a mistake. And, Camila, you noticed.

(4/10/92)

Anne's praise of Camila's correction signaled the teacher's willingness to acknowledge her own mistakes. Thus making mistakes is treated as a normal part of the process of writing. Anne is demonstrating that writers need to be readers, revising their products as they work. In group writing, this is work that is collaborative and shared by students and teacher alike.

Still, the power of the pen is mighty, and the teacher in teacher-led group writing is the one holding the pen. In the following exchange, Montrel calls attention to this power:

(1)   ANNE: OK, I think we did a good job. I'm going to keep this list, so we can come back to it when we decide on the title for our whole book. (Children start clapping.)
(2)   MONTREL: We didn't write it.
(3)   ANNE: I didn't write it, you wrote it.
(4)   MONTREL: We told you to write it, but you wrote it.
(5)   ANNE: Ready set. Get yourselves together. Much better. Now stay that way until I tell you what the next activity is. Cause I didn't know how long it would take. I'm going to go back and look for a book, and while I do that, I'm going to have Montrel come up and read his poem [that he had written earlier in his journal].

(4/10/92)

This is a fascinating point that Montrel has brought up: How much authority did the student authors really have, since the teacher was holding the pen? Anne addresses his concern the first time and credits the students with authorship (turn 3). Montrel, however, will not be deterred and makes his point again, acknowledging Anne's response, but insisting that the act of writing the words on paper carries a certain measure of power that he knows the students did not share in this exercise (turn 4). Anne does not continue this conversation but changes the subject, moving into her role as head of classroom process: speaking as director and boss. She makes an interesting move, though, and gives Montrel the floor (turn 5) to read the poem he had written in his journal. It is possible that this was a way to acknowledge a time when he was clearly the undisputed writer.

Teachers who seek to change their relationships with students for both process and knowledge must understand that this is (in Anne's words) "ongoing": subject to rethinking and revision, much like the writing process itself. Even though this work of restructuring and reordering the students' and teachers' relationships to knowledge and one another is "ongoing" and full of frustrations and challenges, it is also exhilarating at times. That so much of the group writing that occurred in Anne's class was "spontaneous" and arose from student initiations means that children developed a sense that people write for a purpose. It was because students' intentions and purposes were acknowledged and built upon in group writing that they were able to constantly generate authentic reasons to write. The group writing, then, emerged in many cases out of a felt need to communicate. This is well illustrated by an event that Anne related to the parents gathered for the end of the year "Celebration of Learning":

> Something really neat happened today. It's Mr. Lopez's birthday and right away the students came in and said, "We wanna make him a birthday card." And it wasn't even part of my plan. They initiated the fact they wanted to write for a reason, for a birthday card. Part of that's what we did this year. Teaching them that writing and reading are for good reasons. And to make them life-long lovers of reading and writing too. (6/10/92)

CUED ELICITATION

The writing of the birthday card for the principal grew out of student initiations, as did the majority of the group-composed texts throughout the year. However, there were occasions when Anne came with a specific agenda and genre in mind through which to lead the students. Sometimes she put this agenda on hold, as with the writing of the turkey stuffing ingredients. On one occasion, however, Anne's agenda was so strong and clear that the talk surrounding the group composition was very teacher-controlled and did not promote the type of student initiation, cross-discussion, or student evaluation that was usually seen. It is helpful here to analyze the differences in the discourse during this lesson, as it vividly portrays the ways in which student input changes during group composing if the teacher has a fixed idea of how it is the text should read. This, then, is the third discourse pattern, that of "cued elicitation."

The day after a trip to the Brookfield Zoo, Anne decided that the class could write a book about their trip, with each sequenced chapter relating different parts of the visit. The following excerpt is a portion of the 25 minutes of class time devoted to writing the first chapter, which Anne had already decided was to be about spring:

(1)   ANNE: I think this morning we should spend a little time and do some writing about yesterday. Now, one of the things that we—when we first got there, before we even looked at anything, we were discovering something. We saw something, we talked about it. Maya you did. I remember your voice. Anybody remember? . . What we talked about? . . On the tram? We looked at things, what were we looking for? Look, she has her hand up. (No one answers.)

(2)   ANNE: Maybe you don't remember exactly.

(3)   CHILD 1: Tulips

(4)   ANNE: The flowers, are they blooming yet?

(5)   CHILDREN: <u>Yes</u>/
               <u>No</u>

(6)   ANNE: We saw little yellow flowers that weren't in bloom. I gave them another name. What did I call them? Miriam has her hand up.

(7)   MIRIAM: (Lots of hesitancy and silence) I remember you were telling us . . . the bird.

(8)   ANNE: The bird (with much enthusiasm). What was the bird's name?

(9)   CHILDREN: Robins

[Conversation goes on and then continues]

(28)   ANNE: What did we see?

(29)   MONTREL: We didn't see everything.

(30)   ANNE: We didn't quite see everything. Hands up. What do you think of our first chapter being/

(31)   ADRIAN: The dolphin show

(32)   ANNE: No, what did we talk about before we got to the dolphin show? We were riding the tram. We were looking for . . .

(33)   CAMILA: Green

(34)   ANNE: We were looking for robins, the green grass and tulips, the whole thing is called . . .

(35)   CHILDREN: Green

(36)   ANNE: I'm going to put this picture up.

(37)   LATOYA: It's a bear and flowers.

(38)   ANNE: And this kind of flower is called a what?

(39)   MELINDA: Tulip

(40)   ANNE: This is what it's going to look like when it blooms. We saw them when they were about this high. We didn't see the little blooms yet. I'm going to keep looking in my backyard. Mine are up about that high.

(41)   MAYA: I don't have a backyard.

(42)   ANNE: Ready, set, listen. Adrian. Now, so, chapter one/

(43) ADRIAN: The dolphins
(44) ANNE: It's not going to be the dolphins cause we're not there yet.
        What was the first thing we did? We looked for . . (points to word
        spring in poem up on board)
(45) CHILDREN: Spring

(4/10/92)

After 45 turns of talk, the students finally come up with the word that Anne
had been trying to elicit from them: *spring*. She had previously decided that the
first chapter of the book should be about spring. At lunch that day, she told me
what she had been thinking:

> I'd thought about it and decided to do the chapters sequentially. They loved
> the birds. I think they thought they were trapped in the zoo. I don't think
> they know they're just out there and flying around. Then we saw all those
> robins. And the grass was so green.

This excerpt provides such a contrast to the usual form of discourse during group-
composed writing because the students did not engage in any cross-discussion at
all. Furthermore, only the teacher provided evaluatory feedback. Adrian's initiations and responses about the dolphins were not accepted as appropriate to the
topic, and Maya's personal comment about not having a backyard was ignored.

Anne even brought out a picture to try to prompt the students to use the word
for which she was waiting (turn 36). To get the word *spring* from them, she finally
had to resort to pointing to it on the board (turn 44). This example offers an opportunity to examine a style of discourse that Edwards, D., and Mercer (1987)
call "cued elicitation," in which the teacher asks questions while providing clues
to the information wanted:

> The best interpretation that we can make of the pedagogic function of cued elicitation
> is that it embodies an educational process in which the pupils are neither being drawn
> out of themselves . . . nor simply being taught directly, in the 'transmission' sense. . . .
> It is a device which requires that the pupils actively participate in the creation of shared
> knowledge, rather than merely sit and listen to the teacher talking. (p. 143)

The transcriptions from earlier excerpts during group-composed writing offer
examples of talk in which students are "drawn out of themselves" as well as ones
in which the teacher is transmitting information. This excerpt is different from
either of these.

Students' answers were short and hesitant, and Anne's questions were ones to
which she already knew the answer. Therefore the opportunities for students to
share authority with the teacher for what counted as knowledge were limited by

Anne's tight control of what answers would be considered correct. This points toward the importance of balancing both teacher and student agendas in group composing. If the teacher has already decided the topic and structure of the text, she or he has *authored* it ahead of time. This leaves students the job of guessing the correct answers, rather than making original contributions. Thus the floor was not open to student initiations, but rather the teacher was looking for student responses that fit her agenda.

It is important in this analysis to understand Anne's objectives for this lesson. She was introducing a thematic unit on spring and wanted to check for student understandings. A year later, upon reviewing the transcript, Anne explained her goals:

> When we were walking in the zoo I spent quite a bit of time showing them all those things. I wanted them to see the daffodils, tulips, birds. It was hard for some of them to understand that some birds are caged and some are free. Underlying all that was my determination for the sequence of the whole trip. They were excited about dolphins, but I wanted them to put it all down and not just one aspect of it. (6/3/93)

They ended up writing the following piece:

Spring Is Nice
The birds fly. It's spring.
Spring is wonderful.
Spring makes people happy.
Robins like spring. Robins like to fly a lot.
Spring brings the green grass.
Tulips are growing in spring at the zoo.
Tulips are very nice flowers.
The birds are in the trees.

They went on throughout the week to co-author other chapters, including one on the dolphin show. Thus Anne's objectives were met by this exercise: Students used the word *spring* and specific names of birds and flowers associated with it. The final text, however, was a product not of student initiation but of teacher initiation. The words were chosen by the teacher and used by the students only after much cuing from Anne. By having a preset agenda for the content of group-composed writing, then, the teacher did not allow openings for student initiations that were in conflict with her own agenda. Anne did, however, scaffold the students' use of the vocabulary she wanted them to use. Thus the possibilities realized for sharing authorship and authority during group writing varied according to the teacher's agenda.

This chapter has portrayed three types of discourse patterns evidenced during teacher-led group-composed writing. Each offers varying degrees of opportunity for student initiation and sharing of authority. Each also offers teachers different ways to share their own expertise and knowledge. All offer ways for students and teacher to engage in a co-construction of meaning, building a storehouse of common knowledge and shared understandings. Often the people in Room 104 seemed like dancers to me: moving at different speeds around the dance floor of the classroom. In transmission discourse the teacher is the dance instructor, stopping the dancers on the floor to call their attention to specific steps she knows and thinks they can learn also. In cued elicitation the teacher is the paid dance partner, carefully cuing the partner's steps so that they conform to social understandings. And in discourse that leaves the floor wide open to student initiations, the dance is a impromptu one, in which all dancers' interpretive steps are woven together to create an original and unique display.

9

Sharing Authority in the Classroom

I ran into Maya one day after school when she was in second grade. She had come to Anne's room to borrow books on her way home. I asked her how things were going in school and she said, "Pretty good."

"Do you get to read and write much?" I asked.

"Yeah, we have journals."

Then she paused and looked appraisingly around her old first-grade, where the small desks were clustered into groups of four or five. "You know," she continued, "this year we *have* small groups, but we're not *for* small groups." The corners of her mouth turned down, and she looked like she might burst into tears. We talked a little more and it became clear what Maya meant: Exploratory talk with other children about books and writing was not part of the second-grade curriculum. And she knew the difference and missed it.

This book has examined the relationships among students, their teacher, and authority over the course of one school year. By examining the talk during various literacy routines, I have sought to investigate shifting relationships of power and control for classroom process as well as knowledge. When teachers act on the belief that students construct their own understandings and do this as part of a social process that is mediated by both students and teacher, the work and talk in classrooms are bound to change. For to build on student understandings, the teacher must begin by making room for student initiations.

KEY ASPECTS OF SHARING AUTHORITY

While student initiations ebbed and flowed throughout all the classroom routines, the students and teacher grew to be dancers in my mind: catching one another's eyes as they passed in their circles around the room, often following their partner's lead, sometimes carefully scrutinizing another's dance, occasionally dancing to a rhythm only they could hear. In the rest of this chapter, I identify essential aspects of shared authority in the classroom. I offer these as a possible framework for teachers and researchers who want to investigate the dance of shared authority in other classrooms at other times.

The Teacher Actively Shares Her Expertise

The teacher in this classroom not only knew more dances than her students but was also broadly knowledgeable about the music played. In fact, by selecting the texts for Room 104, Anne chose the music which provided an important context for the students' creation of new steps of their own. This is an important expertise that the teacher brings to every educational exchange. As has been shown throughout this book, the teacher is a more expert member of the sociocultural world and must share this expertise with students directly, honestly, (as) accurately (as possible), and persuasively. It is not enough for the teacher to understand choices writers have for genre; the students must learn this also. The teacher directly teaches the skills students need and does not withdraw and make them discover everything for themselves. Anne selected her read-aloud texts carefully: balancing for both information books and fiction, as well as easy-to-read books that students could pick up and read on their own. This book selection also extended to monitoring students' selections for their personal reading: making sure that each student was successful as well as challenged. In this way, teachers must find ways to connect their understandings with the approximations of young children taking gigantic steps and becoming literate.

Teachers also need expertise in group process. They work to keep the students engaged, focused, and on the topic. They must watch the clock and the calendar, striving to meet a range of goals throughout the day and year. Teachers must exert their expertise and must balance participation rights among students, working to draw out quiet students and intercede in peer disputes. Further, they must foster and encourage students to do this for their peers and for themselves as well, as this is fundamental to a participatory democracy. Finally, teachers are the experts in charge of offering invitations for each student, treating individuals differently and contingently responding to all students' initiations in a way that both supports and challenges them. They must feed their students' enthusiasm for joining a literate community and must scaffold their steps into this community. Thus the teacher's expertise is essential and wide-reaching.

Students Initiate for Process and Knowledge

Yet teachers' expertise must be tempered with moments to listen to their students as they share their own expertise. It is here that the teacher stops leading the dance and learns how to follow. It is essential that students sometimes be allowed to speak as experts, both for classroom process and knowledge. They must be initiators of their own questions that can launch purposeful inquiries about a world that is constantly changing; and they must be changers, too, initiating and directing classroom procedures to learn how to act upon the world with authority. There were numerous occasions throughout this study in which student initiations were reflected in the dialogue and actions of the class. Students not only often directed the move from one classroom routine to another; they created new routines as well. They actively managed their own and one another's reading as audience members and readers during child-led read-alouds, as well as by finding specific books and sharing them during buddy reading. Students took an active role in initiating during teacher-led read-alouds, both directing Anne as reader and contributing their knowledge in discussions. They made connections among the text, their personal experiences, and other books, eagerly asserting their right and ability to make sense of their world as they integrated new knowledge. The students took one another seriously, listening to one another's ideas during various classroom routines, engaging in cross-discussion, and building on the ideas of others. They supported one another's struggles to make meaning in writing, responding thoughtfully to one another's writing, laughing at the funny parts and clapping at the end. Quite simply, student initiations throughout the year provide ample evidence that authority for both classroom process and knowledge was shared by students across the curriculum and throughout the year.

A Shared Agenda Is Fundamental

It is essential that these student initiations not be seen as an end product in and of themselves, as these initiations did not emerge into a vacuum. They were negotiated with the teacher, who sometimes ignored them, usually acknowledged them, and frequently took them up. Sometimes this meant that Anne changed her own agenda and followed student initiations instead—remember, for instance, when students read journals instead of writing a recipe for stuffing. The times that Anne put her own agenda on hold—for instance, when she began to explain about the pin pilots wear and the children began to read the book—point toward the underlying premise of shared authority: A sharing of authority is founded on a mutually constructed and common agenda. In this classroom, students' excitement about reading and writing fit with Anne's agenda that they become literate. "I like the fact that I'm the one that brings them into reading" (4/17/91), she told me. And Marcos confided, "Books are my best friends" (5/29/92). This shared agenda worked to build a basis for a growing body of shared understanding and common knowledge. As Dyson (1993) puts it: "To be viable, a singular classroom culture will need to be formed through a kind of *alchemy*, through creating an official classroom world that intersects among many" (p. 216; emphasis added). Students and teacher were co-constructors of a shared knowledge and culture, as they danced in and out of the classroom routines discussed in this book. Often students worked without the teacher, as in shared reading, and brought their own private understandings to the group—as reflected by Montrel's comment, "Me and Marcos know." Anne worked to link these students' discoveries into the large-group discussion, thus feeding the body of shared knowledge with the work of the individual members as well as the group. Thus part of the teacher's expertise is directing the co-construction of meaning as the class steadily builds a foundation of shared understandings. It is the teacher's important role, then, not only to articulate that there is a shared agenda, but to deepen it as well.

Shared Authority Extends Teacher Authority

By allowing and encouraging student initiations and expertise, Anne actually deepened and extended her authority; a teacher who listens to students learns what understandings they bring to the classroom and what matters to them as people. Such a teacher can then use this information to build upon: both in cognitive ways and to facilitate students' growth as purposeful, directed, and intentional learners. By opening the floor to student initiations, teachers become that much more expert about their students, expanding their view of students' strengths and needs. Furthermore, by permitting students to participate fully in shaping the work of the class, teachers can rely more and more on students' willingness and ability to work with one another and give feedback to peers, freeing themselves of the responsibility of being the *sole* evaluator of process and knowledge.

Finally, teachers who share authority become authorities on their own teaching and evaluators of their own work. As Anne explained:

> I look at my authority in a different way now. I know that I'm in stages. I know I can try anything, whether it works or not. I know that I have to read more of what the experts say, but I know that I'm becoming an expert, too—in the sense that I drive my curriculum and instruction much more than I ever have. And it's quite a feeling, quite a good feeling. (1/22/92)

LOOKING BEYOND

This study of shared authority served to clarify and deepen both Anne's and my understandings of the tensions and dilemmas of teacher and student authority in this one classroom. But, ultimately, I want to do research that contributes to making classrooms places for active inquiry for students and teachers. I want to support teachers as they create opportunities for students to be outspoken, articulate, and critical. I want children to grow up believing they can know, find out, persuade, dream, and act decisively and generously upon the world. I want students to believe that they have every right to build communities that make room for all members not only to act on their own initiatives but also to submit these initiatives to the construction of a common agenda with the people around them.

These processes of active inquiry, co-construction of meaning, and group decision making are central to the possibilities of participatory democracy. I do not want to suggest, however, that classrooms can be sites of unhierarchical egalitarian relationships; rather, classrooms can be places where children are inducted into the formal knowledges of the culture(s) and where they can participate in the co-construction of these knowledges as well. Of course, there is nothing inherently liberatory about this. Inviting people to participate in agenda setting and knowledge production does not necessarily ensure that they will use these liberties in ways that foster toleration for ambiguity, empathy for difference, and respect for democratic inquiry. The specific content of these knowledges introduced by the teacher, taken up by the students, and co-constructed by the class can help students critique issues of social justice and democracy, or they can work to obscure them.

So, too, can the processes of sharing classroom authority work toward emancipating and/or colonizing children. By employing pedagogies, such as interactive read-alouds, that often invite student initiations into the classroom conversation, teachers do, however, set in motion new ways to circulate power. Thus the teacher who invites student initiations has to decide how to respond to these initiations. When teachers do not understand or do not value the initiations of their students, potential for great damage exists. For example, in research on sharing-time narratives (Cazden, Michaels, & Tabor, 1985), children's oral stories during show-and-tell were rated differently by Black and White teachers. The more episodic narratives of some of the African American children in the study were understood more easily, and rated higher, by African American adults than by European American adults. Hence, when children are given the floor, but then negatively critiqued for how they use it, the negative effect of teacher power in this otherwise "liberatory" approach becomes obvious. Thus it is imperative to be aware of how we respond to student initiations; our responses are informed in large part by our cultural and social positionings. Student initiations can be used to limit children as well as to liberate them.

In this and many other ways, teachers should not be seen as giving up their power when they share it. In fact, what I have termed *sharing authority* is quite problematic, as it suggests that authority is a possession that can be broken into pieces and given away to students. What I have tried to illustrate through classroom examples is that even when students are able to initiate and direct classroom process and knowledge, the teacher has not given up her or his power, authority, position, or privilege. Rather, how these are deployed has shifted, causing new problems for the teacher and new behaviors to regulate.

Make no mistake about it, teachers—whether embracing holistic and democratic pedagogies or not—regulate student behaviors for the intended purpose of regulating or unleashing (depending on one's perspective) learning. When, however, the teacher moves toward pedagogies that foster student dialogue, discussion, and initiation, the ways in which teacher and student authorities are negotiated also shift. There can be no simple formula for teachers traversing this murky terrain. As seen by the excerpts of classroom talk from Room 104, when to step in as leader, and when to step back as follower and facilitator, is an ongoing dance.

I originally conceptualized sharing authority as always walking a fine line— wiggling a little this way one moment, and then back again the next. I thought of it as a balancing act: moving in and out of student initiations and teacher expertise. I am not so sure now that authority can ever be pinned down and straddled so neatly as one would attempt, for instance, on a balance beam. Rather, teacher and students continue to circle round and round each other, inserting themselves and asking to be heard, demanding to enter the flow of classroom life.

Teachers who invite students to share authority for classroom process and knowledge are inviting them to contribute directly to the movement and direction of classroom experiences. They can examine in what ways they can open the floor to student initiations. They can search for ways to acknowledge these initiations and decide when and how to build upon them. Teachers can notice when they take up student initiations and when peers do so as well. They can make this process metacognitive, pointing explicitly to the ways in which students are working together to build not only a shared community and shared understandings, but contested terrain as well.

Teachers can reflect on the ways in which their own expertise provides scaffolding for student learning and thereby make their responses contingent on student understandings. They can decide when to step in with this expertise and lead the dance of the classroom, what music to play, and how best to teach new dance steps. And then, teachers can listen as their students bring new music into the classroom which they themselves have never even heard. They can watch students create new movements, listening to their rhythms and trying to learn both *from* them and *with* them. In this process, teachers must not abdicate their authority in an attempt to share it. But rather, we must work with our students to teach them the established dances, learn their new ones, and together with our mutual expertise create new dances the world has yet to see.

Afterword

"What I'm always doing is thinking, thinking, just thinking things through. Where I have come from? What am I doing? Where was I last year?" These are my own words spoken to Celia, and even though they were spoken a little more than four years ago, this is something that I will always do as my students and I continue to share authority. Thus I believe I should change all the "I's" to "we."

Where have these first graders and I come from? What are we doing? Where, then, is this first-grade class of the school year 1991–92 as this book is being written? The mobility rate for Jungman School is high. There are perhaps 9 students presently attending Jungman School (school year 1995–96) out of the original 23 students in Room 104. Of course, it's fun to see them in the halls and to kind of check in on how they are doing. I sense that their growth in literacy is developing and expanding so that they may continue to act upon their own initiatives. It is in the sharing of authority within literacy activities and routines that they will acquire the life-long desire of being readers, writers, and learners.

There is also a dimension attached to this shared authority that I have very recently become aware of. At the beginning of this school year, before the students had arrived, the Jungman teachers were involved in various staff development activities and programs. As I was exiting the front door on one of these days, I could hear two of my students from the previous year, who lived nearby, yelling to me from across the street. They were bike riding and in a flash had come across the street to say "Hi!" Immediately after that came "I need a hug!" from one of them. What struck me about this request was that had this student not been in my class, perhaps I might never have heard those words. Why? When we share authority with our students, we are truly sharing ourselves. Just as our students need the process—me, in sharing authority about the classroom procedures (the who, what, when)—they also need the sharing of content. When you respect the knowledge of young children in interactive literacy routines, what also comes through is the sharing of ourselves. Although most children have fond memories of their first-grade teachers, I believe that if I did not open up the classroom to student initiations, questions, needs, and desires, then I would not have students feeling free and open enough to ask for a hug. It is in our openness to friends and to be who we really are that our personal selves can be connected despite the fact that we are so different in so many ways. For me, this is the most important aspect of sharing authority.

Even to be able to go about changing traditional teaching theories and practices and to try this New Literacy required the openness of my principal, Fausto Lopez, who let me take the risks, the support of my Jungman colleagues; the help and advice of Christine Pappas, University of Illinois at Chicago professor; and last but not least—Celia Oyler. I feel so fortunate that I just happened to be the teacher in the right place at the right time. Celia exemplifies the thoughts and words she has written concerning university researchers sharing authority with teachers such as I. We worked in a relationship that was supported and encouraged by each other. This is her study of my new adventure. I cannot thank her enough for her encouragement and enthusiasm as I was wrestling with sharing authority and changing my teaching practices and theories.

This new adventure has become an ongoing, many-layered experience as I look upon myself as a teacher-researcher as well as a teacher learning from professional development and along with and from my students.

I have really learned the value of the construction of knowledge as it has enabled me to look at other teachers and to experience their models for what works and is possible in the classroom. Participating in national conferences such as the National Council of Teachers of English and the National Reading Conference generates knowledge. This forms a basis for teacher inquiry and action-research forever.

What is it like as a professional to be able to come to the realization that there is for me a different relationship with the children that I teach? I am still constantly amazed at what my students know. Their initiations that happen through shared authority are the impetus that keeps my inquiries ongoing.

By opening up my classroom to student questions, comments, thoughts, ideas, beliefs, opinions, and feelings, I am able to listen and to look at how my students are connecting to the real world. No matter what grade in school, students need to be listened to and responded to.

Vivian Gussin Paley listened with her tape recorder to children for many years because of her curiosity to learn more about the students she was teaching. She feels that when we are curious about a student's words and our responses to those words, then the student feels respected and is respected. I, too, am very curious about my students' voices. I can never predict what they will say and am fascinated by their responses. My greatest challenge, then, is to keep trying to connect what my students already know to what they don't know.

Sharing authority always seems to come back to making connections. What my students and I have done, what we do, and what we will do makes an impact not only on each other, but also on the people in our lives.

Anne Barry
Jungman School
Chicago, Illinois

Notes on Method and Methodology

DATA COLLECTION

The first part of the study (January through May, 1991) consisted of the weekly teachers' meeting on using an integrated language perspective, led by Christine Pappas; I was an active participant in these conversations. During this time I conducted individual, semistructured interviews with all of the teachers in the group, including Anne. These meetings and interviews were recorded. I transcribed chunks of these tapes pertaining to teacher change and urban issues during the summer of 1991. I listened to all of these tapes again in the winter of 1992–93 and transcribed additional conversations.

The second part of the study ran from October 1991 through June 1992. During this time, a smaller subset of the teachers' group continued to meet—usually five or six women—and these weekly conversations were again recorded. Additionally, I began working as a participant–observer in Anne Barry's first-grade classroom. I made some visits without collecting data, merely to be a part of the classroom (for instance, the day I helped the students make gingerbread figures). I made 22 formal full-day visits to the classroom, taking field notes and audiorecording throughout the day.

I used one microphone, which was able to pick up most whole-class activities. During activities that were not large-group ones, I left the microphone either in a small group of students or asked Anne to carry it with her as she floated from student to student. Children helped in this process, often calling my attention to a tape that needed turning over or requesting that I record them read. In my field notes I recorded nonverbal communication and actions, as well as writing as much as was possible of particular conversations I felt were significant.

Conversations between Anne and me were sandwiched in throughout the day and were also recorded. We talked before school, in the hallways walking the children to lunch and the bathroom, during her 20-minute lunch break, and sometimes after school. I transcribed chunks of the recorded classroom tapes immediately after each visit, focusing on excerpts that illustrated aspects of shared authority. I merged these transcriptions with my field notes from the day.

Classroom artifacts were collected by photographing teacher- and student-made products on chalkboards and bulletin boards. Additionally, I photocopied samples of student journals and other writing projects.

At the end of the school year I also transcribed sections of the audiotapes from the meetings with the teachers; I focused on exchanges that dealt with teacher authority, Anne's reflections on her own development, and questions she posed regarding making the shift toward what she called more holistic methods. Also at the end of the year, I listened to the classroom tapes again and transcribed additional parts.

The third phase of data collection continued up until June 1993 and involved ongoing analysis of all data. Using the transcriptions and field notes from the classroom, from conversations with Anne, and from the two years of teachers' meetings, I marked themes relating to shared authority across the data sources. These were shared and discussed with Anne, and her reflections were recorded and also used as data. Further data later included conversations between Anne and me as we prepared for professional presentations and papers; these were recorded and parts were transcribed.

USING DISCOURSE ANALYSIS

A significant part of data analysis in this study involved examining the discourse, or talk, of the classroom. Studies of classroom discourse have generally come from two different perspectives: either process–product or sociolinguistic (Cazden, 1986). This study is informed by the latter tendency, wherein research is more qualitative and interpretive, influenced by ethnography, the new sociology of education (M. Young, 1971), and interactive sociolinguistics (Sinclair & Coulthard, 1975). As Green, Kantor, and Rogers (1991) explain:

> Language at the discourse level is language in use and, thus, it involves the discourse strategies and social actions employed by participants as they work together verbally and nonverbally to accomplish their goals for this "bit of social life" (p. 342).

Since I was interested in examining the ways in which teacher and students worked together to create, negotiate, and attain their goals, an analysis of the actual discourse provided a way to investigate how authority was constructed in this classroom. This is not to imply, however, that the utterances recorded and transcribed are transparent indicators of power and authority. Rather, the talk of the classroom is seen as a window into examining how authority was and was not shared. Language, after all, is the "primary content and means of education" (Bloome & Bailey, 1992, p. 181). Teacher's language choices in the classroom control not only the process but also the flow of knowledge (Edwards, A. D., 1980; Hunter, 1980). As R. Young (1992) has noted:

> Teacher utterances are a manifold claim. Either the relational claim that a teacher makes on a learner is completely and ubiquitously dominant, to the detriment of other valid-

ity claims, or the claims of the pupil as an apprentice co-inquirer are given some weight and the relational claim of cognitive authority and trust that the teacher may make is made with restraint. Either the pupil will be a pedagogical object or a developing fellow citizen of our one world. (p. 88)

Specific interpretations were made, then, of the comments of teacher and students that pointed toward the establishment and negotiation of authority. Yet even in the process of deciding which comments to record, which recordings to transcribe, and which transcriptions to use, there is an enormous amount of researcher subjectivity. As noted in *Researching Language*: "Research inevitably involves the recontexualisation of utterances and so even the most deliberate discourses are likely to be reinterpreted" (Cameron, Frazer, Harvey, Rampton, & Richardson, 1992, p. 132). It should be understood, then, that as a researcher I bring all of my own positionings both to the classroom observations and to the interpretations on the page.

THEORY-BUILDING RESEARCH

It used to be traditional in educational research to address issues of validity and generalizability. These, however, are not relevant constructs for this study because I do not seek to address the general, nor make predications for the general either. As Bloome and Bailey (1992) have noted:

Rather than seeking universals there is an increasing emphasis on the particular: on what happens in a particular place, at a particular time, with a particular set of people, engaged in a particular activity and event. What becomes important about that particular place, time, people, activity and event, is what it means, what its significance is for the people involved and for others, and what its import is for other events. (p. 182)

From this study of one particular classroom and teacher, I offer a tentative framework with which to view other classrooms. So if there is generalizability, it lies with the reader to search for how generic and stable these processes are for other places and other times (Erikson, 1992).

Finally, the eclectic methods utilized in this study—it is not a linguistic discourse analysis or a contextually developed ethnography—suggest that any conclusions offered be taken as insights rather than findings (Edwards, A. D., & Westgate, 1994). After all, I have listened, watched, recorded, transcribed, and presented events and conversations that caught my interest in pursuit of theory building around the concept of shared authority.

Transcription Format

Transcripts are presented in the text as conversations, using a new line for each new speaker. Although these conversational turns are certainly not so neatly marked on the audiotapes, they are displayed in an edited format for ease of reading. A turn was considered to be a string of utterances spoken between other people's utterances (Sacks, Schegloff, & Jefferson, 1974) and is transcribed with each turn displayed under the previous turn. Listed below are more detailed explanations of transcription notation.

Punctuation	Periods, exclamation marks, and question marks have been added for ease of reading.
Layout	In some dialogues, every time a new person begins a speaking turn, this utterance is sequentially numbered.
Child 1	If the name of the child speaking is not known, the speaker is identified with a number. The same voice is given the same number during each excerpt.
Capitals	Words in all capital letters are words from a text being read out loud.
/	Indicates interruption
(. . .)	Indicates undecipherable comments
. . .	Indicates a pause—the more dots, the longer the pause
_____	Utterances that overlap are underlined
Italics	Indicates words heavily emphasized
[ ]	Statements inside brackets are explanations or provide additional information.
( )	Statements inside parentheses provide observations or action recorded in field notes.

References

Alpert, B. R. (1987). Active, silent and controlled discussion: Explaining variations in classroom conversations. *Teaching and Teacher Education, 3*, 29–40.

Anyon, J. (1980). Social class and the hidden curriculum of work. *Journal of Education, 162*, 67–92.

Apple, M. (1982). *Education and power.* Boston: Routledge & Kegan Paul.

Arendt, H. (1968). *Between past and future: Eight exercises in political thought.* New York: Viking.

Atwell, N. (1987). *In the middle: Writing, reading, and learning with adolescents.* Montclair, NJ: Boyton/Cook.

Ayers, W., & Schubert, W. H. (Eds.). (1992). *Teacher lore: Learning from our own experience.* White Plains, NY: Longman.

Barnes, D. (1990). Language in the secondary classroom. In D. Barnes, J. Britton, & M. Torbe (Eds.), *Language, the learner and the school* (pp. 9–88). Portsmouth, NH: Heinemann.

Bernstein, B. (1990). *Class, codes and control: Vol 4. The structuring of pedagogic discourse.* London: Routledge.

Bloome, D., & Bailey, F. (1992). Studying language and literacy through events, particularity, and intertextuality. In R. Beach, J. L. Green, M. L. Kamil, & T. Shanahan (Eds.), *Multidisciplinary perspectives on literacy research* (pp. 181–210). Urbana, IL: National Conference on Research in English.

Bloome, D., & Egan-Robertson, A. (1992). *The social construction of intertextuality in classroom reading and writing lessons.* Unpublished manuscript.

Bourdieu, P. (1973). Cultural reproduction and social reproduction. In R. Brown (Ed.), *Knowledge, education, and cultural change* (pp. 71–112). London: Tavistock.

Bourdieu, P., & Passeron, J. C. (1977). *Reproduction in education, society and culture.* Beverly Hills, CA: Sage.

Bowles, S., & Gintis, H. (1976). *Schooling in capitalist America.* New York: Basic Books.

Bruner, J. S. (1985). Vygotsky: A historical and conceptual perspective. In J. V. Wertsch (Ed.), *Culture, communication and cognition: Vygotskian perspectives* (pp. 21–34). New York: Cambridge University Press.

Bruner, J. S. (1986). *Actual minds, possible worlds.* Cambridge, MA: Harvard University Press.

Calkins, L. (1983). *Lessons from a child.* Portsmouth, NH: Heinemann.

Calkins, L. (1986). *The art of teaching writing.* Portsmouth, NH: Heinemann.

Cameron, D., Frazer, E., Harvey, P., Rampton, M. B. H., & Richardson, K. (1992). *Researching language: Issues of power and method.* New York: Routledge.

Canter, L., & Canter, M. (1976). *Assertive Discipline: A take charge approach for today's educator*. Seal Beach, CA: Canter & Associates.

Carlsen, W. S. (1991). Questioning in classrooms: A sociolinguistic perspective. *Review of Educational Research, 61*, 157–178.

Cazden, C. (1986). Classroom discourse. In M. Wittrock (Ed.), *Handbook of research on teaching* (pp. 432–463). New York: Macmillan.

Cazden, C. (1988). *Classroom discourse: The language of teaching and learning*. Portsmouth, NH: Heinemann.

Cazden, C., Michaels, S., & Tabor, P. (1985). Spontaneous repairs in sharing time narratives: The intersection of metalinguistic awareness, speech event, and narrative style. In S. W. Freedman (Ed.), *The acquisition of written language* (pp. 51–64). Norwood, NJ: Ablex.

Chicago Public Schools. (1992). *Annual School Report Card*. Chicago: Chicago Public Schools.

Chicago Public Schools. (1992–93). *News and notes*. Chicago: Department of Language and Cultural Education.

Christie, F. (1989). Language development in education. In R. Hasan & J. R. Martin (Eds.), *Language development: Learning language, learning culture. Meaning and choice in language: Studies for Michael Halliday* (pp. 152–198). Norwood, NJ: Ablex.

Clandinin, D. J., Davies, A., Hogan, P., & Kennard, B. (Eds.).(1993). *Learning to teach, teaching to learn: Stories of collaboration in teacher education*. New York: Teachers College Press.

Cochran-Smith, M. (1991). Learning to teach against the grain. *Harvard Educational Review, 61*, 279–310.

Connelly, F. M., & Clandinin, J. (1990). Stories of experience and narrative inquiry. *Educational Researcher, 19*(5), 2–14.

Cremin, L. (1961). *The transformation of the school: Progressivism in American education 1876–1957*. New York: Random House.

Davies, B. (1993). *Shards of glass: Children reading and writing beyond gendered identities*. Cresskill, NJ: Hampton.

Delamont, S. (1983). *Interaction in the classroom* (2nd ed.). New York: Methuen.

Delpit, L. D. (1988). The silenced dialogue: Power and pedagogy in educating other people's children. *Harvard Educational Review, 58*, 379–385.

Dewey, J. (1938). *Experience and education*. London: Collier-Macmillan.

Dickinson, D., & Keebler, R. (1989). Variations in preschool teachers' storybook reading styles. *Discourse Processes, 12*, 353–376.

Dillon, J. T. (1985). Using questions to foil discussion. *Teaching and Teacher Education, 1*, 109–121.

Doake, D. B. (1985). Reading-like behavior: Its role in learning to read. In A. Jaggar & M. T. Smith-Burke (Eds.), *Observing the language learner* (pp. 82–98). Newark, DE: International Reading Association.

Dunning, D., & Mason J. (1984, November). *An investigation of kindergarten children's expressions of story characters' intentions*. Paper presented at the annual meeting of the National Reading Conference, St. Petersburg, FL.

Dyson, A. H. (1989). *Multiple worlds of child writers: Friends learning to write*. New York: Teachers College Press.

Dyson, A. H. (1993). *Social worlds of children learning to write in an urban primary school*. New York: Teachers College Press.

Edelsky, C. (1991). *With literacy and justice for all: Rethinking the social in language and education*. New York: Falmer.

Edelsky, C., Draper, K., & Smith, K. (1983). Hookin' 'em in at the start of school in a "whole language" classroom. *Anthropology and Education Quarterly, 14,* 257–281.

Edwards, A. D. (1980). Patterns of power and authority in classroom talk. In P. Woods (Ed.), *Teacher strategies* (pp. 237–253). London: Croom Helm.

Edwards, A. D., & Westgate, P. G. (1994). *Investigating classroom talk* (3rd ed.). London: Falmer.

Edwards, D., & Mercer, N. (1987). *Common knowledge: The development of understanding in the classroom*. New York: Routledge.

Ellsworth, E. (1989). Why doesn't this feel empowering?: Working through the repressive myths of critical pedagogy. *Harvard Educational Review, 59,* 297–324.

Erikson, F. (1992). Why the clinical trial doesn't work as a metaphor for educational research: A response to Schrag. *Educational Researcher, 21,* 9–11.

Farrar, M. T. (1988). A sociolinguistic analysis of discussion. In J. T. Dillon (Ed.), *Questioning and discussion: A multidisciplinary study* (pp. 29–73). Norwood, NJ: Ablex.

Flanders, N. A. (1970). *Analyzing teacher behavior*. Reading, MA: Addison-Wesley.

Forman, E., & Cazden, C. (1985). Exploring Vygotskian perspectives in education: The cognitive value of peer interaction. In J. Wertsch (Ed.), *Culture, communication and cognition: Vygotskian perspectives* (pp. 323–347). Cambridge, England: Cambridge University Press.

Foucault, M. (1980). *Power/knowledge: Selected interviews and other writings, 1972–1977* (C. Gordon, Ed. & Trans.). New York: Pantheon.

Freire, P. (1970). *Pedagogy of the oppressed* (M. B. Ramos, Trans). New York: Seabury.

Freire, P. (1994, Spring). On education and the taste for democracy. *The Writing Instructor,* pp. 116–120.

Gee, J. P. (1987). What is literacy? *Teaching and Learning: The Journal of Natural Inquiry, 2*(1), 3–11.

Getzels, J. W. (1975). Problem-finding and the inventiveness of solutions. *Journal of Creative Behavior, 9,* 12–18.

Gilbert, P. (1991). *Fashioning the feminine: Girls, popular culture and schooling*. Sydney, Australia: Allen & Unwin.

Giroux, H. (1988). Literacy and the pedagogy of voice and political empowerment. *Educational Theory, 38,* 61–75.

Giroux, H., & McLaren, P. (1986). Teacher education and the politics of engagement. *Harvard Educational Review, 56,* 213–238.

Gitlin, A. (1990). Educative research, voice, and school change. *Harvard Educational Review, 60,* 443–466.

Goodman, J. (1992). *Elementary schooling for critical democracy*. Albany: State University of New York Press.

Goodman, K. (1986). *What's whole in whole language?* Portsmouth, NH: Heinemann.

Gore, J. M. (1993). *The struggle for pedagogies: Critical and feminist discourses as regimes of truth*. New York: Routledge.

Gore, J. M. (1994, April). *Power and pedagogy: An empirical investigation of four sites.*

Paper presented at the annual meeting of the American Educational Research Association, New Orleans, LA.

Gore, J. M. (1995, January). *On the continuity of power relations in pedagogy.* Paper presented at the International Sociology of Education Conference, Sheffield, England.

Graves, D. (1983). *Writing: Teachers and children at work.* Portsmouth, NH: Heinemann.

Green, J. L., Kantor, R. M., & Rogers, T. (1991). Exploring the complexity of language and learning in classroom contexts. In L. Idol & B. F. Jones (Eds.), *Educational values and cognitive instruction: Implications for reform* (pp. 333–364). Hillsdale, NJ: Erlbaum.

Grumet, M. (1988). *Bitter milk: Women and teaching.* Amherst: University of Massachusetts Press.

Hammersley, M. (1977). School learning: The cultural resources required by pupils to answer a teacher's question. In P. Woods & M. Hammersley (Eds.), *School experience: Explorations in the sociology of education* (pp. 167–213). New York: St. Martin's Press.

Heath, S. B. (1983). *Ways with words: Language, life and work in communities and classroom.* Cambridge, England: Cambridge University Press.

Heron, J. (1981). Philosophical basis for a new paradigm. In P. Reason & J. Rowan (Eds.), *Human inquiry: A sourcebook of new paradigm research* (pp. 19–35). New York: Wiley.

Holdaway, D. (1979). *The foundations of literacy.* Sydney, Australia: Ashton Scholastic.

Hollingsworth, S., & Minarik, L. T. (1991, April). *Choice, risk and teacher voice: Closing the distance between public perceptions and private realities of schooling.* Paper presented at the annual meeting of the American Educational Research Association, Chicago.

Hollingsworth, S., Teel, K., & Minarik, L. (1992). Learning to teach Aaron: A beginning teacher's story of literacy instruction in an urban classroom. *Journal of Teacher Education, 43,* 116–127.

Horwitz, R. A. (1979). Psychological effects of the "open classroom." *Review of Educational Research, 49,* 71–86.

Hunter, C. (1980). The politics of participation—with specific reference to teacher-pupil relationships. In P. Woods (Ed.), *Teacher strategies* (pp. 213–236). London: Croom Helm.

Hymes, D. H. (1982). What is ethnography? In P. Gilmore & A. A. Glatthorn (Eds.), *Children in and out of school: Ethnography and education* (pp. 21–32). Washington, DC: Center for Applied Linguistics.

Hynds, S. (1994). *Making connections: Language and learning in the classroom.* Norwood, MA: Christopher-Gordon Publishers.

Johnston, M. (1990). Experience and reflections on collaborative research. *Qualitative Studies in Education, 3,* 173–183.

Jungman School Team. (1992, May). *From time to time: A proposal to restructure time for future planning* (Proposal submitted to the Chicago Public Schools). Chicago.

Klein, A. M. (1989). Meaningful reading and writing in a first-grade classroom. *The Elementary School Journal, 90,* 184–192.

Kohl, H. (1976). *On teaching.* New York: Bantam.

Kozol, J. (1991). *Savage inequalities.* New York: Crown.

Kreisberg, S. (1992). *Transforming power: Domination, empowerment, and education.* Albany: State University of New York Press.

Lather, P. (1991). *Getting smart.* New York: Routledge.

Lemke, J. (1990). *Talking science: Language, learning, and values.* Norwood, NJ: Ablex.

Lensmire, T. (1994). *When children write: Critical re-vision of the writing workshop.* New York: Teachers College Press.

Lewin, K. (1944). The dynamics of group action. *Educational Leadership, 1*(4), 195–200.

Luke, A. (1991). The political economy of reading instruction. In C. D. Baker & A. Luke (Eds.), *Towards a critical sociology of reading pedagogy* (pp. 3–25). Philadelphia: John Benjamins Publishing.

Manke, M. (1990). *Constructing power relationships.* Unpublished doctoral dissertation, University of Virginia.

Manke, M. (1991, October). *When humility is required: The stance of the teacher in the student-centered classroom.* Paper presented at the Bergamo Conference on Curriculum Theory and Classroom Practice, Dayton, OH.

Manke, M. (1993, April). *Sally, would you like to sit down?: Teachers using indirect discourse strategies, including politeness formulas.* Paper presented at the annual meeting of the American Educational Research Association, Atlanta, GA.

Martinez, M. G., & Teale, W. H. (1993). Teacher storybook reading style: A comparison of six teachers. *Research in the Teaching of English, 27,* 175–199.

McCollum, P. (1989). Turn-allocation in lessons with North American and Puerto Rican students: A comparative study. *Anthropology and Education Quarterly, 20,* 133–156.

McLaren, P. (1989). *Life in schools: Introduction to critical pedagogy in the foundations of education.* White Plains, NY: Longman.

Mehan, H. (1979). *Learning lessons.* Cambridge, MA: Harvard University Press.

Miller, J. L. (1990). *Creating spaces and finding voices: Teachers collaborating for empowerment.* Albany: State University of New York Press.

Moll, L. C. (1992). Literacy research in community and classrooms: A sociocultural approach. In R. Beach, J. L. Green, M. L. Kamil, & T. Shanahan (Eds.), *Multidisciplinary perspectives on literacy research* (pp. 211–244). Urbana, IL: National Council of Teachers of English.

Newman, J. (1985). *Whole language: Theory in use.* Portsmouth, NH: Heinmann.

Newman, J. (1991). Teacher talk: Learning to teach by uncovering our assumptions. In D. Booth & C. Thornely-Hall (Eds.), *The talk curriculum* (pp. 107–122). Portsmouth, NH: Heinemann.

Nikola-Lisa, W. (1992). Read aloud, play a lot: Children's spontaneous responses to literature. *The New Advocate, 5,* 199–213.

Oyler, C. (1996). Sharing authority during teacher-led read-alouds of information books. *Teaching and Teacher Education, 12*(2).

Oyler, C., & Barry, A. (1992, December). *Sharing authority during teacher-led read-alouds: Alternatives to the IRE.* Paper presented at the National Reading Conference, San Antonio, TX.

Oyler, C., & Barry, A. (1993, December). *Urban first graders intertextual connections in the collaborative talk around information books during teacher-led read-alouds.* Paper presented at the National Reading Conference, Charleston, SC.

Oyler, C., & Becker, J. (1993, October). *Sharing authority: Between a rock and a soft place*. Paper presented at the Annual Conference on Curriculum Theory and Classroom Practice, Dayton, OH.

Oyler, C., & Pappas, C. C. (1992, October). *Claiming and sharing our authority in collaboration*. Paper presented at the annual Conference on Curriculum Theory and Classroom Practice, Dayton, OH.

Pagano, J. A. (1990). *Exiles and communities: Teaching in the patriarchal wilderness*. Albany: State University of New York Press.

Pappas, C. C., Kiefer, B. Z., & Levstik, L. S. (1990). *An integrated language perspective in the elementary school: Theory into action*. White Plains, NY: Longman.

Pappas, C. C., Kiefer, B. Z., & Levstik, L. S. (1995). *An integrated language perspective in the elementary school: Theory into action* (2nd ed.). White Plains, NY: Longman.

Peterman, C. L., Dunning, D., & Mason, J. (1985, December). *A storybook reading event: How a teacher's presentation affects kindergarten children's subsequent attempts to read from the text*. Paper presented at the annual meeting of the National Reading Conference, San Diego.

Peters, R. S. (1966). *Ethics and education*. London: Allen & Unwin.

Pimm, D. (1987). *Speaking mathematically: Communication in mathematics classrooms*. London: Routledge & Kegan Paul.

Plowden, B. (1967). *Children and their primary schools*. London: Her Majesty's Stationery Office.

Postman, N., & Weingartner, C. (1969). *Teaching as a subversive activity*. Harmondsworth, England: Penguin.

Rhodes, L. K. (1979). "I can read": Predictable books as resources for reading and writing instruction. *Reading Teacher, 34*, 511–518.

Richman, L. S. (1990, April 9). The coming world labor shortage. *Fortune*, pp. 70–77.

Routman, R. (1988). *Transitions: From literature to literacy*. Portsmouth, NH: Heinemann.

Routman, R. (1990). *Invitations: Changing as teachers and learners K–12*. Portsmouth, NH: Heinemann.

Sacks, H., Schegloff, E., & Jefferson, G. (1974). A simplist systematics for the organization of turn-taking in conversation. *Language, 50*, 696–735.

Shor, I., & Freire, P. (1987). *A pedagogy for liberation: Dialogues on transforming education*. South Hadley, MA: Bergin & Garvey.

Sinclair, J. M., & Coulthard, R. M. (1975). *Towards an analysis of discourse: The English used by teachers and pupils*. London: Oxford University Press.

Smith, F. (1982). *Writing and the writer*. New York: Holt, Rinehart & Winston.

Spring, J. (1991). *American education: An introduction to social and political aspects*. White Plains, NY: Longman.

Stenhouse, L. (1975). *An introduction to curriculum research and development*. London: Heinemann.

Stock, P., & Robinson, J. (1989). Literacy and conversation: Classroom talk as text building. In D. Bloom (Ed.), *Classrooms and literacy* (pp. 310–368). Norwood, NJ: Ablex.

Stodolsky, S. (1988). *The subject matters: Classroom activity in math and social studies*. Chicago: University of Chicago Press.

Stubbs, M. (1976). *Language, schools, and classrooms*. London: Methuen.

Sudol, D, & Sudol, P. (1991). Another story: Putting Graves, Calkins, and Atwell into practice and perspective. *Language Arts, 68*, 292–300.

Sulzby, E., & Teale, W. (1987). Emergent literacy. In D. Bloome (Ed.), *Literacy and schooling* (pp. 727–753). Norwood, NJ: Ablex.

Swadener, B. B., & Lubeck, S. (Eds.). (1995). *Children and families "at promise": Deconstructing the discourse of risk.* Albany: State University of New York Press.

Teale, W. H., Martinez, M. G., & Glass, W. L. (1989). Describing classroom storybook reading. In D. Bloome (Ed.), *Classrooms and literacy* (pp. 158–188). Norwood, NJ: Ablex.

Temple, C., Nathan, R., Burris, N., & Temple, F. (1988). *The beginnings of writing.* Boston: Allyn & Bacon.

Tierney, R. J., & Rogers, T. (1989). Exploring the cognitive consequences of variations in the social fabric of classroom literacy events. In D. Bloome (Ed.), *Classrooms and literacy* (pp. 250–263). Norwood, NJ: Ablex.

Vygotsky, L. S. (1978). *Mind in society: The development of higher psychological processes.* Cambridge: Harvard University Press.

Walkerdine, V. (1990). *Schoolgirl fictions.* New York: Verso.

Wartenberg, T. E. (1990). *The forms of power: From domination to transformation.* Philadelphia: Temple University Press.

Watson, D. J. (1989). Defining and describing whole language. *The Elementary School Journal, 90*, 129–141.

Wells, G. (1981). *Learning through interaction: The study of language development.* New York: Cambridge University Press.

Wells, G. (1986). *The meaning makers: Children learning language and using language to learn.* Portsmouth, NH: Heinemann.

Wells, G., & Chang-Wells, G. L. (1992). *Constructing knowledge together: Classrooms as centers of inquiry and literacy.* Portsmouth, NH: Heinemann.

White, J. J. (1989). The power of politeness in the classroom: Cultural codes that create and constrain knowledge construction. *Journal of Curriculum and Supervision, 4*, 98–321.

Willinsky, J. (1990). *The New Literacy: Redefining reading and writing in the schools.* New York: Routledge.

Willis, P. (1977). *Learning to labor: How working class kids get working class jobs.* New York: Columbia University Press.

Wood, D., Bruner, J. S., & Ross, G. (1976). The role of tutoring in problem solving. *Journal of Child Psychology and Child Psychiatry, 17*, 89–100.

Wood, D., & Wood, H. (1988). Questioning versus student initiative. In J. T. Dillon (Ed.), *Questioning and discourse: A multidisciplinary study* (pp. 280–305). Norwood, NJ: Ablex.

Young, M. (1971). *Knowledge and control: New directions in the sociology of education.* New York: Macmillan.

Young, R. (1992). *Critical theory and classroom talk.* Clevedon, England: Multi-lingual Matters.

Children's Literature Cited

Ahlberg, J., & Ahlberg, A. (1986). *The Jolly Postman*. Boston: Little, Brown.

Ahlberg, J., & Ahlberg, A. (1991). *The Jolly Christmas Postman*. Boston: Little, Brown.

Appleby, E. (1985). *Three billy goats gruff*. New York: Scholastic.

Arnold, C. (1990). *A walk by the seashore*. New York: Simon & Schuster.

Behrns, J. (1978). *Fiesta*. San Francisco: Golden Gate.

Booth, J., Booth, D., Pauli, W., & Phenix, J. (Eds.). (1984). *How I wonder*. Toronto: Holt, Rinehart & Winston of Canada.

Butler, A. (1984). *Excuses, excuses*. Crystal Lake, IL: Rigsby.

Carter, D. (1991). *In a dark, dark wood*. New York: Simon & Schuster.

Carter, D. (1992). *Over in the meadow*. New York: Scholastic.

Cowley, J. (1980). *Mrs. Wishy-Washy*. Bothell, WA: The Wright Group.

De Bourgoing, P. (1991). *The tree*. New York: Scholastic.

Drew, D. (1987). *The book of animal records*. Crystal Lake, IL: Rigsby.

Gibbons, G. (1989). *Monarch butterflies*. New York: Holiday.

Heller, R. (1981). *Chickens aren't the only ones*. New York: Scholastic, Inc.

Ingoglia, G. (1991). *Look inside the earth*. New York: Putnam.

Lester, H. (1988). *Tacky the penguin*. New York: Houghton Mifflin.

Lobel, A. (1970). *Frog and toad are friends*. New York: Harper & Row.

Lobel, A. (1971). *Frog and toad together*. New York: Harper & Row.

Martin, B., & Archambault, J. (1989). *Chicka chicka boom boom*. New York: Simon & Schuster.

McKie, R., & Eastman, P. (1962). *Snow*. New York: Random House.

McPhail, D. (1987). *First flight*. New York: Little, Brown.

McQueen, L. (1985). *Little red hen*. New York: Scholastic.

Munsch, R. (1986). *Love you forever*. Buffalo, NY: Firefly.

Munsch, R., & Kusugak, M. (1988). *A promise is a promise*. Buffalo, NY: Firefly.

Neville, P., & Butler, A. (1984). *Green bananas*. Crystal Lake, IL: Rigsby.

Parkes, B., & Smith, J. (1984). *The gingerbread man*. Crystal Lake, IL: Rigsby.

Patterson, D. (1991). *Koko's kitten*. New York: Scholastic.

Rey, H. A. (1941). *Curious George*. New York: Houghton Mifflin.

Rey, H. A. (1943). *Where's my baby?*. New York: Houghton Mifflin.

Sendak, M. (1962). *Chicken soup with rice: A book of months*. New York: HarperCollins.

Seuss, D. (1963). *Hop on pop*. New York: Random House.

Stevenson, J. (1986). *Fried feathers for Thanksgiving*. New York: Green Willow.

White, E. B. (1952). *Charlotte's web*. New York: Harper & Row.

Wiseman, B. (1959). *Morris the moose*. New York: HarperCollins.

Index

Affective response, 53, 64–65
Agenda, shared, 134–135
Ahlberg, A., 41, 75–76
Ahlberg, J., 41, 75–76
Alpert, B. R., 21
Anyon, J., 5, 28, 29
Apple, M., 28
Appleby, E., 81
Archambault, J., 42, 96
Arendt, H., 6
Arnold, C., 58
Assertive Discipline, 45–47
At-home journals, 114–115
Atwell, N., 4, 99
Authority
  abdicating or claiming, 23–25
  among researchers, 16
  and "buddy" system, 7, 87–98
  classroom process, 35, 40–47, 132–137
  extending, 37
  and power, 22–27
  shared. *See* Shared authority
  teacher, 5, 20–22, 99–100, 123–124, 135
Ayers, W., 16

Bailey, F., 142, 143
Barnes, D., 8, 20, 21, 55, 63, 112
Barry, Anne, vii, 1–6, 8, 10, 15–18, 19, 31,
  50, 52, 70, 72, 127–131, 139–140
Becker, J., 24
Behrns, J., 59, 68–69
Bernstein, B., 6
Bloome, D., 60–63, 142, 143
Book of Animal Records, The (Drew), 58–59
Book read-alouds, 75–83
Booth, D., 79, 121
Booth, J., 79, 121
Bourdieu, P., 6, 28
Bowles, S., 28

Bruner, Jerome S., 25, 56
Buddy reading, 87–90
Burris, N., 99
Butler, A., 100, 118

Calkins, Larry, 4, 99, 103, 105–106, 115
Cameron, D., 143
Canter, L., 45
Canter, M., 45
Carlsen, W. S., 21
Carter, D., 33–34, 92
Cazden, C., 5, 13, 21, 26, 89, 136, 142
Center for Research in Urban Education, 12
Chang-Wells, G. L., 8, 23, 26, 66–67, 125
Charlotte's Web (White), 105–106
Chicago School Reform Act of 1988, 2, 10–11
Chicka Chicka Boom Boom (Martin and
  Archambault), 42, 96
Chickens Aren't the Only Ones (Heller), 52–
  53, 61–62
Chicken Soup with Rice (Sendak), 121–122
Child-led read-alouds, 7, 14, 39–40, 72–86
Christie, F., 22, 57
Clandinin, D. Jean, vii–x, 16
Classroom process
  and Assertive Discipline, 45–47
  authority in, 35, 40–47, 132–137
  class schedules in, 34–35
  and control, 43–45
  negotiating classroom work, 41–43
Cochran-Smith, M., 29
Collaborative approach, 5, 16
Common Knowledge (Edwards and Mercer), 27
Competition, 80–81
Connelly, F. M., 16
Constructivist approach, 3, 25–27
Control
  author, in journal writing, 100–103
  in the classroom, 43–45

Coulthard, R. M., 142
Cowley, J., 94
Cremin, L., 15
Cued elicitation, in group-composed writing, 127–131
Curious George (Rey), 77

Data analysis, for study, 15–16
Data collection, for study, 14–15, 141–142
Davies, A., 16
Davies, B., 108
De Bourgoing, P., 57
Delamont, S., 20, 21
Delpit, Lisa D., 17, 28, 105, 125
Democracy, 3, 134–135
Dewey, Alice Chapman, 15
Dewey, John, 2, 3, 15
Dickinson, D., 50
Dillon, J. T., 21
Direct transmission, in group-composed writing, 124–127
Discipline, Assertive, 45–47
Discourse analysis, for study, 14, 142–143
Discovery learning, 26
Doake, D. B., 20, 89–90
Donadt, M., vii–viii
Draper, K., 16
Drew, D., 58
Dunning, D., 50
Dyson, Anne H., 8, 74, 134

Eastman, P., 76
Edelsky, C., 16, 24
Editing journals, 115–116
Edwards, A. D., 5, 20, 21, 22, 142, 143
Edwards, D., 5, 13, 21, 26, 27, 59, 63, 67, 91–92, 102, 117, 123, 129
Egan-Robertson, A., 60–63
Ellsworth, E., 25
Emancipatory pedagogy, 25
Erikson, F., 143
Ethnographic techniques, 14
Excuses, Excuses (Butler), 118
Experience, personal, 53, 56–59
Expertise
    claiming, 53, 63–64
    of teacher, 65–71, 133

Farrar, M. T., 21
Feminist theory, 15–16

Fiesta (Behrns), 59–60, 68–69
First Flight (McPhail), 36, 67–68
Flanders, N. A., 21
Forman, E., 5
Foucault, M., 6, 22, 23
Frazer, E., 143
Freire, Paulo, 2–3, 20, 24, 25, 86
Fried Feathers for Thanksgiving (Stevenson), 36–37

Gee, J. P., 28
Genre, changes in, 104–112
Getzels, J. W., 55
Gibbons, G., 60
Gilbert, P., 108
Gingerbread Man, The (Parkes and Smith), 62–63
Gintis, H., 28
Giroux, H., 17–18, 25
Gitlin, A., 16
Glass, W. L., 50–51
Goodman, J., 24, 26
Goodman, K., 4
Gore, J. M., 6, 22
Graves, D., 4, 99
Green, J. L., 142
Green Bananas (Neville and Butler), 100
Greene, Maxine, 31, 49
Group-composed writing, 8, 14, 117–131
    cued elicitation in, 127–131
    direct transmission of, 124–127
    student evaluation of, 121–124
    student initiation of, 118–124
    teacher authority in, 123–124
Grumet, M., 22

Hammersley, M., 55
Harvey, P., 143
Heath, S. B., 17
Heller, R., 52, 61
Heron, J., 15, 16
Hogan, P., 16
Holdaway, D., 87
Hollingsworth, S., 16
Hop on Pop (Seuss), 1, 7, 84–85
Horwitz, R. A., 26–27
How I Wonder (Booth, et al.), 43, 79
Hunter, C., 3, 5, 19, 20, 21, 142
Hymes, D. H., 14
Hynds, S., 58

In a Dark, Dark Wood (Carter), 33–34
Ingoglia, G., 63
Intertextual links, 53, 59–61
IRE (initiation/response/evaluation) model, 13, 26, 51–52

Jefferson, G., 144
Johnston, M., 16
Jolly Christmas Postman, The (Ahlberg and Ahlberg), 76
Jolly Postman, The (Ahlberg and Ahlberg), 41
Journal read-alouds, 72–75
Journal writing, 7–8, 14, 32–34, 99–116
    and at-home journals, 114–115
    author control in, 100–103
    editing and revising in, 115–116
    and genre changes, 104–112
    read-alouds and, 72–75
    as social process, 112–114
    spelling and, 99–100
    teacher authority in, 99–100
Jungman School
    mobility rate of, 139
    neighborhood of, 9–10
    and school reform, 10–11
    teacher profile, 12

Kantor, R. M., 142
Keebler, R., 50
Kennard, B., 16
Kiefer, B. Z., 3, 103
Klein, A. M., 3
Knowledge
    and shared authority, 6, 21, 133–134
    teacher, 65–71, 133
Kohl, H., 5
Koko's Kitten (Patterson), 64–65
Kozol, J., 5
Kreisberg, S., 20, 22, 23
Kusugak, M., 69

Lather, P., 15
Leadership, of children, 85–86
Lembec, Jay, 13
Lemke, J., 21, 56, 120
Lensmire, Timothy, 4, 74, 105, 108
Lester, H., 81
Levstik, L. S., 3, 103
Lewin, K., 15
Little Red Hen (McQueen), 98

Lobel, A., 61–62
Local School Councils (LSCs), 11
Look Inside the Earth (Ingoglia), 63–64
Lopez, Fausto, 140
Love You Forever (Munsch), 70
Lubeck, S., 5
Luke, A., 24

Magnet schools, 80
Manke, M., 24, 33, 89, 96, 102, 114
Martin, B., 42, 96
Martinez, M. G., 50–51
Mason, J., 50
McCollum, P., 57, 58
McKie, R., 76
McLaren, P., 25, 27
McPhail, D., 36, 67
McQueen, L., 98
Mehan, H., 5, 13, 21, 26
Mercer, N., 5, 13, 21, 26, 27, 59, 63, 67, 91–92, 102, 117, 123, 129
Michaels, S., 136
Miller, J. L., 16
Minarik, L., 16
Mrs. Wishy Washy (Cowley), 94
Moll, L. C., 5
Monarch Butterflies (Gibbons), 60
Morris the Moose (Wiseman), 93–94
Munsch, R., 69–70

Nathan, R., 99
Neville, P., 100
New Literacy, 2, 3, 16, 19, 101, 140
Newman, J., 4, 122
Nikola-Lisa, W., 51

Over in the Meadow (Carter), 92
Oyler, C., 4, 15, 16, 24, 50, 52, 140

Pagano, C. C., 15
Pagano, Jo Anne, 39, 99, 101, 109
Paley, Vivian Gussin, 140
Pappas, Christine C., 3, 12, 24, 87, 94, 103, 117–119, 124–125, 140
Parents, reactions to shared authority, 47–49
Parkes, B., 62
Passeron, J. C., 6
Patterson, D., 64–65
Pauli, W., 79, 121
Personal experience, 53, 56–59

Peterman, C. L., 50
Peters, R. S., 13, 21
Phenix, J., 79, 121
Piaget, Jean, 25
Pimm, D., 64, 95
Plowden, B., 25
Postman, N., 55
Power
    and authority, 6, 21, 22–27
    teacher, 5
Primary School movement, 25–26
Project CANAL (Creating A New Approach to
        Learning), 11
Promise Is a Promise, A (Munsch and
        Kusugak), 69–70

Questions
    student, 53, 54–56
    teacher, 21

Rampton, M. B. H., 143
Read-alouds. *See also* Shared reading
    book, 75–83
    child-led, 7, 14, 39–40, 72–86
    journal, 72–75
    teacher-led, 7, 14, 36–37, 50–71
Reading
    moving from journal writing to, 33–34
    shared, 7, 14, 37–39, 87–95
Reflective practice, ix
Researching Language (Cameron et al.),
        143
Revising journals, 115–116
Rey, H. A., 77
Rhodes, L. K., 93
Richardson, K., 143
Richman, L. S., 28
Robinson, J., 105
Rogers, T., 13, 22, 94, 142
Ross, G., 25
Rote learning, 5
Routman, Regie, 3–4, 103, 125

Sacks, H., 144
Scaffolding, 25, 47–48, 67, 91
Schedules, class, 34–35
Schegloff, E., 144
Schoolgirl Fictions (Walkerdine), 27
Schubert, W. H., 16
Sendak, M., 121
Seuss, D., 1, 7, 84

Shared authority, ix, 4, 5–6, 13
    for classroom process, 40–47, 132–137
    key aspects of, 132–135
    and knowledge, 6, 21, 133–134
    and power, 6, 21
    and social class, 17, 27–29
    and teacher education, 29–30
Shared reading, 7, 14, 37–39, 87–90
    and buddy reading, 87–90
    peer interactions in, 90–95
Shor, Ira, 24, 25
Sinclair, J. M., 142
Smith, F., 99
Smith, J., 62
Smith, K., 16
Snow (McKie and Eastman), 76
Social class, and shared authority, 17, 27–29
Spelling, and journal writing, 99–100
Spring, J., 29
Stenhouse, L., 15, 22, 44–45
Stevenson, J., 36–37
Stock, P., 105
Stodolsky, S., 26, 94
Stubbs, M., 21, 55
Student evaluations, in group-composed
        writing, 121–124
Student initiations, 51–63
    affective response, 53, 64–65
    balancing teacher expertise with, 65–71
    claiming expertise, 53, 63–64
    and classroom control, 43–45
    directing process, 52–54
    in group-composed writing, 118–124
    intertextual link, 53, 59–61
    moving from journal writing to reading,
        33–34
    personal experience, 53, 56–59
    questioning for understanding, 53, 54–56
    reading text, 52–54
    in shared authority, 133–134
    teacher initiations versus, 105–108
    in writing, 105–108
Students, read-alouds led by, 7, 14, 39–40,
        72–86
Sudol, D., 4
Sudol, P., 4
Sulzby, E., 68
Swadener, B. B., 5

Tabor, P., 136
Tacky the Penguin (Lester), 81

Teacher(s)
  authority of, 5, 20–22, 99–100, 123–124,
     135
  balancing expertise with student initiations,
     65–71
  education of, and shared authority, 29–30
  expertise of, 65–71, 133
  and IRE model, 13, 26, 51–52
  negotiation of peer interaction in shared
     reading, 92–95
  profile of, 12
  questions of, 21
  read-alouds led by, 7, 14, 36–37, 50–71
Teale, W. H., 50–51, 68
Teel, K., 16
Temple, C., 99
Temple, F., 99
Three Billy Goats Gruff (Appleby), 81
Tierney, R. J., 13, 22, 94
Tree, The (De Bourgoing), 57–58

Vygotsky, L. S., 25

Walk by the Seashore, A (Arnold), 58–59
Walkerdine, V., 6, 22, 27, 28

Wartenberg, T. E., 6, 22–23
Watson, D. J., 70
Weingartner, C., 55
Wells, G., 8, 20, 23, 26, 66–67, 120, 125
Westgate, P. G., 143
When Children Write (Lensmire), 74
Where's My Baby? (Rey), 77
White, E. B., 105–107
White, J. J., 89
Whole-class texts, 81–83
Whole-language approach, 2, 24
Willinsky, J., 2, 4, 16, 19, 24, 70, 100–101,
     108
Willis, P., 26, 28
Wiseman, B., 93
Wood, D., 21, 25, 51
Wood, H., 21, 51
Writing
  group-composed, 8, 14, 117–131
  journal, 7–8, 14, 32–34, 99–116
  student initiation of, 105–108
Writing-process approach, 24

Young, M., 142
Young, Robert, 16, 20, 54, 142–143

About the Author

Celia Oyler is Assistant Professor of Education in Teaching and Leadership at Syracuse University, where she teaches in the Inclusive Elementary and Special Education Program. She taught for 15 years in public and alternative schools in Chicago, Vermont, Connecticut, and, most recently, Syracuse, New York. She received a B.S. in Special Education from Southern Connecticut State College, an M.Ed. in Consulting Teaching from the University of Vermont, and a Ph.D. in Curriculum and Instruction from the University of Illinois at Chicago. Her research focus is on instructional practices that support democratic schooling, critical democracy, and full inclusion.